CONNECTING THE
SUPERNATURAL

CONNECTING THE
SUPERNATURAL

LANRE AHMED FATAI

AuthorHouse™
1663 Liberty Drive
Bloomington, IN 47403
www.authorhouse.com
Phone: 1-800-839-8640

Published by AuthorHouse 11/17/2014

ISBN: 978-1-4969-5161-8 (sc)
ISBN: 978-1-4969-5162-5 (hc)
ISBN: 978-1-4969-5160-1 (e)

Library of Congress Control Number: 2014919770

All Bible quotations in this book are from the King James Version unless otherwise stated.

Scripture quotations marked KJV are from the Holy Bible, King James Version (Authorized Version). First published in 1611. Quoted from the KJV Classic Reference Bible, Copyright © 1983 by The Zondervan Corporation.

CONTENTS

DEDICATION

I wish to dedicate this book to the memory of all
those who were killed—and are being killed—
in fulfillment of the prophecy in John 16:2.

*They shall put you out of the synagogues; yea the time cometh,
that whosoever killeth you will think that he doeth God service.*

Especially those killed during bomb attacks on
various worship centers across the country. May
their souls find eternal rest in Jesus's name.

ACKNOWLEDGMENTS

Let me begin by first acknowledging the Almighty God whom I call the Absolute God, for His mercies endure forever. Also with abiding gratitude for the many who have positively influenced me during my Christian formative years, I wish to acknowledge four of them who made significant contributions in areas of my greatest needs.

Bishop David Oyedepo, the founder Living Faith Churches worldwide (Winners' Chapel). You taught me the principles of living a practical Christian life.

Dr. Kola, E-Matthew, like Moses to Joshua, God called me through you and made me see what is possible with Him in the kingdom.

Bishop TD Jakes, though we have never met physically, you taught me deep things of God through your Holy Spirit–led teachings.

Bishop Duncan Philip, my spiritual father, your guidance and insightful mentoring through the years, provided me with the platform to serve God.

My profound appreciation and love goes to Pastor (Mrs.) Georgina Ahmed for being my wife and the mother of my sons (King-David Oluwaseun and Daniel Oluwaseyi). I sincerely appreciate your love, perseverance, and motherly care for our children and me. You are indeed a treasure. To my adopted daughters (Eniola and Busola), you are deeply loved.

Freedom Chapel family, I say a big thank you. You are wonderful people of God. To all my friends out there, including Brother Rasak

Osere, you helped by reading this work. God bless you all. My continual prayer is that when the trumpet sounds, we will all meet with Him in the sky and live with Him forever in the kingdom of His Father in Jesus's mighty name. Amen.

INTRODUCTION

The supernatural represents the realm of the spirit where forces beyond human comprehension shape the destinies of many. Actions already accomplished in the supernatural are manifested in the natural and are seen as the destiny of people. In other words, virtually all the important and significant things that happen in the life of a person are preceded by unseen actions in the realm above the natural. These actions are invisible to the mortal and can only be discerned in the spirit. The Holy Bible makes us to understand:

> That which is born of the flesh is flesh; and that which is born of the spirit is spirit.
>
> —John 3:6

In essence, a person's sojourn in life is not only determined by what the physical eyes can see, but certain actions take place in the realm above the natural and contribute significantly in shaping life. Therefore, a person who lives only in the natural—that is, just by the flesh, without the ability to connect with the supernatural—will be in a helpless and hopeless situation as far as the shaping of his or her destiny is concerned.

God lives and operates in the supernatural. That is why the Bible says those who worship God must worship Him in spirit and in truth. Spiritual things are only discernible in the spirit. One of the greatest disasters that can happen to anyone is hopelessness. Spiritual hopelessness is when a person is living in this world just by the flesh without any connection with the supernatural.

Let me paint a graphic illustration of such hopelessness you can easily relate to. You have a beautiful, sophisticated telephone handset and live in an area where there are highly efficient network service providers. If you fail to get the necessary SIM card from a network provider for your beautiful and sophisticated handset—even though every possibility exists for you to enjoy data and voice services from the service providers through the handset—you will be unable to connect for lack of the bridge (the SIM card). But the moment you get a SIM card—no matter how small it is or if it is a code—you are linked up. You will begin to enjoy every package available from the service providers through your beautiful telephone handset. With the SIM card, your handset is connected to the available packages from the service provider. That way, you will benefit from such packages.

In the same way, a person is in an unproductive state when he or she is not connected with the supernatural. He or she has all the potential and ability that God deposited inside him or her, but the potential and ability cannot be put to effective use without the person being synchronized with his or her maker in the supernatural. However, the moment a link is established with the supernatural, the latent abilities and potentials are stirred up by the creative powers in the supernatural and the person begin to function at full capacity. It is expedient and crucial for you to seek and connect with the supernatural. The supernatural is the place of power and authority. It is the abode of the Almighty God.

Through the leading and help of the Holy Spirit, this book will take you through the simplest route of connecting to this important supernatural. It will enable you to become an active participant in the shaping of your life and destiny. Do you desire to live a fruitful and productive life? Has your life been plagued by stagnation? Are you always the odd person out? You don't like the way life is treating you? You may be asking; why am I not making progress in life? If so, you need this book. Your situation can only turn for the better when you connect with the place of power and authority: the supernatural. Many are the adversaries of men that we need higher authority and power to confront and overcome them. This is only possible when you connect with the supernatural. Apostle Paul through the leading of the Holy Spirit wrote;

> Put on the whole armor of God that ye may be able to stand against the wiles of the devil. For we wrestle not against flesh and blood, but against principalities, against powers, against the rulers of the darkness of this world, against spiritual wickedness in high places.
>
> —Ephesians 6:11–12

Friends, don't be deceived, the kingdom of darkness is constantly waging war against human destiny. The preoccupation of the rulers of the darkness of this world is to see that people did not enter into rest, and it takes putting on the whole armor of God to be able to stand against this onslaught. This can only be achieved when you connect with the supernatural.

Another truth you need to know at this point is that there are treasures in this world. Everything God created was good. However, these treasures are in the deep and hidden in mystery by God. Nothing significant can be found on the surface. It takes the Spirit of God in you to search them out, and by searching it out, you can be a partaker of the blessing.

Life is without form and void in the absence of the Spirit and the Word of God. When the two connect, there is instant transformation. Moses wrote in Genesis; the book of the beginning:

> And the earth was without form and void; and darkness
> was upon the face of the deep. And the Spirit of God
> moved upon the face of the waters. And God said, let there
> be light; and there was light.
>
> —Genesis 1:2–3

The Word of God contains creative powers. The words with these creative powers can only locate your needs through God's Spirit in you. Please don't be left out. God, your maker, does not want you to be left out. The decision and actions needed to be part of the kingdom's blessing rest with you. The good news is that God earnestly desires that you connect the supernatural and partner with Him in realizing the expected end He has pre-paid for you.

> For the earnest expectation of the creature waiteth for the
> manifestation of the sons of God.
>
> —Romans 8:19

God is waiting for your manifestation. His expectation is for you to fulfill your purpose in life. Friend, you are one of the children of God. The scripture says so, and your Creator earnestly awaits your manifestation. What are you waiting for? Take yourself out of hopelessness. Put a stop to the manipulations of the wicked in your life. Stop living only in the natural. Stop leaving your manifestation to the whims and caprices of the devil and his agents. Get involved today, connect with the supernatural, and see things take a new positive turn in your life in the mighty name of Jesus.

I feel sorry when I see people moving from one Prayer Mountain to another or turning themselves into prayer projects. Some have lost hope in God's ability to answer prayers. No! God has not changed. In fact, He does not change—and He will never change. The Bible says He is the same yesterday, today, and forever.

God answered Elijah by fire thousands of years ago, and he is still on the throne today, giving answers to the requests and petitions of the righteous. Take a moment to check things out. Are you connected with the supernatural? It is only when you connect that your prayers become effectual. There is power deposited inside you. This power can only be put to use when you connect with the supernatural. The scripture cannot be broken.

> The effectual fervent prayer of the righteous man availeth much.
>
> —James 5:16b

If you are not experiencing answered prayers at this point in time, it's not that the heavens are closed. God hasn't gone on transfer or holiday. You are probably not connected with the supernatural. Your connection to the supernatural confers righteousness on you, and that is what makes your prayers to avail much. You might be saying, "Wait a minute, Man of God. What are you saying? You just said when I connect with the supernatural, righteousness is conferred on me." Don't get agitated; hold your breath. It is a statement of truth, and you will soon find out about this truth.

To let the cat out of the bag, connecting with the supernatural is about living in faith. Hallelujah. Living with faith in God Almighty. I am talking about the omnipotent and omniscient God: Creator of heaven and earth; Alpha and Omega; the one who cannot be searched out. I personally call this God the Absolute God. He controls the supernatural. The Bible says all powers in heaven, on earth, and beneath are given unto Him. Everything is subject to His control. The three-in-one God: God the Father, God the Son, and God the Holy Spirit. He changes not. He is the same yesterday, today, and forevermore. There is no variableness in Him He is constant and has never failed. He will never fail because He is eternal. This is the God I'm asking you to connect with through faith.

Faith is the connecting bridge to the supernatural. It is the bridge that links your natural with the supernatural. It voided the gap between your natural and the supernatural. It brings you out of darkness into the lights of God and turns your sweat to sweet. Only through faith can you please your Creator, and when your Creator is pleased, you are positioned for His blessings and lifting.

God is waiting to see your faith in action. He will open up His treasure and pour His abundant blessings upon you. Beloved, faith is a requirement for the supernatural to give attention to you. Without faith, life is dull, colorless, and un-interesting. In summary, without it, there is no living.

In this book, I make a bold attempt to expound on what faith represents—how to get it, keeping it jealously, and walking in it—and the benefits thereof. It is written with you in mind, irrespective of your present level of knowledge and walk with God. If you read through this book prayerfully, the Holy Spirit will teach you something through it—and your life will never be the same. God does not fail. He has never failed, and your case will not be different in his mighty name. We have this assurance from the scripture:

> The entrance of thy words giveth light; it giveth understanding to the simple.
>
> —Psalm 119:130

Let this undiluted Word of God be a lamp unto your feet, and it will surely light up your path.

GOD'S AGENDA FOR HUMANKIND

There was something awesome in the mind of God when He was creating you and me. Our coming into this world was not by accident. And it was not by evolution (as scientists want us to believe). We are a deliberate creation of God and have a definite purpose in life. There is a specific reason why you are here.

A specific need exists in this planet that only you can meet. This is the reason why more than five hundred million potential humans competed to come to this world at the same time that you did. But only you made it. In human reproduction, when a male releases sperm, more than five million spermatozoa (potential human beings) race toward the egg for a chance to come into the world. You got there first, and the others lost out because you had a specific assignment to fulfill in the world. You cannot afford to pass through the world without fulfilling your specific purpose. It will be a major disaster if after making it to the world and going through the stiff competition, you lived through life without fulfilling your calling.

Our purpose for coming (our calling) is encapsulated in God's agenda for our lives. It takes a discovery of this agenda to live it out. If you don't know why you are here, you will go through life without focus. You will drift through it like a ball that is tossed by the wind. This is the reason I'm starting this expedition with elaborate explanation of God's purpose and agenda for humankind. Come with me as we explore the scriptures to see what is on God's mind about your life. You will discover that life is good.

Let us begin with the Word of God in Genesis, the book of the beginning. Three distinct actions characterized the creation of people.

Humankind Was Created on Specification

The creation of humankind was remarkably different from the rest of the creatures. God created everything on earth, including the grass, the herb-yielding trees, the fowl of the air, the beast of the field, and other creeping things by speaking His Word. The Word of God has creative powers that brought all the creatures of the earth into being.

> And God said, "Let there be light, and there was light …"
> And God said, "Let there be a firmament in the midst of the waters and let it divide the waters from the waters …"
> And God said "Let the earth bring forth grass, the herb yielding seed, and the fruit tree yielding fruit after its kind, and the tree yielding fruit, whose seed was in itself, after its kind …"
> And God said, "Let the waters bring forth abundantly the moving creature that hath life, and the fowl that may fly above the earth in the open firmament of heaven …"
> And God said, "Let the earth bring forth the living creature after his kind, cattle and creeping things and beast of the earth after his kind; and it was so."
> —Genesis 1:3–24

This is the account of how God created every living creature on the earth. God spoke the Word, and the Word went into action, releasing the creative power in them. However, when it came to the creation of people on the sixth day, there was a deliberation about what people should look like.

God the Father presented a prototype of what people should look like to His creative team of God the Son and God the Holy Spirit. He said let us make people in our image, after our likeness. This suggests to me that in whatever form you came out into this world, you are an expressed image of God. Being short or tall, black or white, thin or fat, bowlegged or straight-legged, man or woman, tribe or race; it doesn't matter. You are an expressed image of God. Take a look at yourself in the mirror; what you see staring back at you is God's likeness. Let nobody or any situation talk you out of this truth. God was very specific about how He wanted you to look.

> And God said let us make man in our image, after our likeness; and let them have dominion over the fish of the sea, and over the fowl of the air, and over the cattle, and over all the earth, and over every creeping thing that creepeth upon the earth. So God created man in his own image, in the image of God created he him; male and female created he them.
>
> —Genesis 1:26–27

Humankind Was Created to Specification

The second thing that happened was that God created people just in line with the prototype that was agreed upon. He formed us exactly the way He proposed to do. There was no mistake or variation at any point. At no point did He change His mind to alter the image of how He wanted you to come out. He took His time to perfect your creation because He knew that when He was done with your creation, there was no other job pending for Him to do—other than rest. You are the perfection of all God's creation. He deployed all His craftsmanship to work for you to come out the way you are.

> For we are his workmanship, created in Christ Jesus unto good works, which God hath before ordained that we should walk in them.
>
> —Ephesians 2:10

Therefore, no matter how you got here—whether your mother had you out of wedlock or you are a child of circumstances—it does not matter. Thank God you are here and open yourself up for His blessings. In fact, you are never a child of circumstance as some want you to believe. Whether your parents were ready or not when they had you, it did not really matter. You are a deliberate creation of God for a specific purpose in life. Don't allow the lies of the devil to rob you of your heritage in life.

Humankind Made a Spirit Being and Blessed

The third definite thing that happened to people during creation was that God put His Holy Spirit in them and blessed them. The Creator breathed His breath on Adam after he was formed out of the dust of the ground and became a living soul.

> And the Lord God formed man of the dust of the ground, and breathed into his nostrils the breath of life; and man became a living soul.
>
> —Genesis 2:7

The breath of God represented His Spirit, and with this breath, God conferred a spirit nature on humankind. Humankind was created as divinity in human form. Unlike other creatures, we carry God's divine nature in us. We were conferred with every nature of God; whatever is possible in God is possible in humankind. Whatever cannot be found in God was not to be found in people.

There was flow of extreme love from God to this creature made by His hand. David captured this flow of love vividly.

> What is man, that thou art mindful of him? And the Son of man, that thou visitest him? For thou hast made him a little lower than the angels, and hath crown him with glory and honor.
>
> —Psalm 8:4–5

God crowned us with glory and honor. From the first day of creation to the fifth day, God was busy creating a throne for humankind. He used His creative words to create the throne called earth. Each time God looked at the throne He was building for humankind and saw anything lacking, He said, "Let there be." And there always be. When He was through with the beautification and provision process of the earth, He brought us in on the sixth day and spoke the Word again to declare His agenda for us.

> And God blessed them, and God said unto them, "Be fruitful, and multiply, and replenish the earth, and subdue it: and have dominion over the fish of the sea, and over the fowl of the air, and over every living thing that moveth upon the earth."
>
> —Genesis 1:28

This set the pace for God's agenda for your life and my life. It serves as the focal point for everything God wants us to be on the surface of the earth. It represents the original plan of God for you and me.

By being fruitful, God is saying we should have abundance in every area of our lives.

Fruit is a collection of many seeds. He said we should multiply, which means we should have speed. Multiplication is different from addition. Addition is slow in progression, but multiplication connotes speed. God gave us speed in everything we do. God created the heavens and the earth—and everything in them—in just six days.

God also said we should replenish the earth, which means we should carry on with further creation on earth. God confers creative ability in people. People can take a tree and create a table out of the raw materials. People can invent and produce things that make life beautiful, good, and comfortable. Above all, this agenda set humankind in dominion above other creatures. We are to be in total control of the environment. We are to have total control of our destinies and be in charge. God gave us each a mind that does not harbor confusion. Our minds are crystal clear about what to do at any given time. Since we carry God's nature, we are never confused. The word of God says:

> "For I know the thoughts that I think toward you," saith
> the Lord, "thoughts of peace, and not of evil, to give you
> an expected end."
> —Jeremiah 29:11

The agenda of God for humankind is born out of an intense love. From the beginning, God fell in love with people and gave them an open check. He handed over the garden that He had meticulously put in place for people to till and look after. You could see the love in the eyes of His adoration toward us. The Bible says He will come in the cool of the day to fellowship with his beloved.

In this agenda, we are expected to flourish in a garden that lacks nothing. God's blueprint for you and me does not contain a proviso for struggles. Struggles are alien in the God's agenda for us.

I cannot locate any agenda where God planned for people to experience fluctuations in their fortunes. It is important for us to have this understanding. We need to put the record straight at this stage so you will have an understanding of what I'm talking about when we begin to deal with issues. It takes understanding an issue to appreciate it. I see your understanding coming alive in Jesus's name.

Key Revelations from the Chapter

- ✓ You are not in this world by accident.
- ✓ You are a deliberate creation of God.
- ✓ There was no mistake in your creation.
- ✓ You are here according to God's plan and desire for your life.
- ✓ God created you for a definite purpose.
- ✓ Your purpose for coming to this world cannot be fulfilled by any other person.
- ✓ In God's agenda for your life, you are to exhibit five characteristics:
  - fruitfulness
  - multiplication
  - replenishment
  - control
  - direction

Notes
My Learning Points

THE DISCONNECT

Something terrible happened to people that altered the course of their destinies and cut them from the glory God had placed him. This unfortunate incident plummeted humankind from the divine great height of love and provision into the abyss of human deprivation. The serpent made people to go against God's instruction. In disobedience to God's instruction, Adam and Eve ate from the tree of the knowledge of good and evil. This disobedience kindled the anger of a disappointed lover (God) who came down in His usual fashion in the cool of the day to fellowship with His beloved only to find His beloved in the embrace of satan. Out of anger, God drove Adam and Eve out of their original place—the supernatural—and disconnected them from this place of power and authority. Humankind's ability to operate in the power and authority of the supernatural was terminated by his disobedience.

> And when the woman saw that the tree was good for food, and pleasant to the eyes, and a tree to be desired to make one wise, she took of the fruit thereof, and did eat, and gave also unto her husband with her; and he did eat.
> And the eyes of them both were opened, and they knew that they were naked; and they sew fig leaves together, and make themselves aprons.

And they heard the voice of the Lord God walking in the garden in the cool of the day; and Adam and his wife hid themselves from the presence of the Lord God amongst the trees of the garden.

And the Lord God called unto Adam, and said unto him, "Where art thou?" …

And unto Adam he said, "Because thou hast hearkened unto the voice of thy wife, and hast eaten of the tree, of which I commanded thee saying thou shalt not eat of it: cursed is the ground for thy sake; in sorrow shalt thou eat of all the days of thy life;

Thorns also and thistles shall it bring forth to thee; and thou shalt eat the herb of the field;

In the sweat of thy face shalt thou eat bread, till thou return unto the ground; for out of it wast thou taken: for dust thou art, and unto dust shalt thou returned".

—Genesis 3: 6–9; 17–19

This unfortunate situation brought the disconnection between humankind (natural) and the divine (supernatural). Humankind could not operate as he ought to be operating. Curse came upon the ground his operational base, and everything went into disarray. The era of struggles, unfulfillment, failure, and every ill that characterizes the earth today are the fall out of the curse. Humankind was driven out of his original place where God has positioned him for his needs to be met without fluctuation.

In the haste of the guilt, Adam left the presence of his Creator with his gaze cast down and descend into the depravity of the natural where satan reigns.

But the intensity of God's love for humankind will not allow God to leave him permanently in this state of hopeleness. God saw that people were too weak to find the way back to Him following the fall in the garden. God begin to plan a way of escape for them. Friend, you can't beat the love of God for you. Despite the fact that Adam and Eve messed up through disobedience, God still made a way to rescue them from the eternal condemnation they have put themselves. God knew fully well that humankind was too weak to come back to God on his own. From this time forward—until Jesus Christ came and went to the cross at Calvary—God unfolded and worked out a rescue mission for humankind. This rescue mission was packaged in blood sacrifice for the remission of sin. Without the blood, there is no remission of sin.

> And almost all things are by the law purge with blood; and without shedding of blood is no remission.
>
> —Hebrews 9:22

Beginning with the blood of bulls and bullocks, God made ways for humankind to come back to God's original plan for their lives. God made it possible for people to come back to his original position by blotting out his sin through blood sacrifice. This was necessary because God is a Holy God. The blood of bulls and bullocks in the Old Testament were shadows of which the shedding of the blood of Jesus in the new covenant was the reality. People cannot come to God in their fallen state; the fragrance of human sin cannot allow them to approach the holy presence of God. God being omniscient sees and knows all things, however, there is one thing God did not know and that is sin; hear this:

> For he hath made him to be sin for us, who knew no sin; that we might be made the righteousness of God in him.
>
> —2 Corinthians 5:21

People falling into sin were not strange to God, for God is an all knowing God. God had already ransomed His only begotten son Jesus Christ from the foundation of the world as appropriation for sin. This eternal truth was revealed to John in the book of revelation.

> And all that dwell upon the earth shall worship him, whose names are not written in the book of life of the Lamb slain from the foundation of the world,
>
> —Revelation 13:8

However, some options of reconciling people back to God were worked out without yielding a permanent solution until the coming of our Lord Jesus Christ. These options include the covenant of the foreskin with Abraham.

God commanded Abraham to circumcise the foreskin of every male child born to him or bought with his money as a token of an everlasting covenant.

> This is my covenant, which ye shall keep. Between me and you and thy seed after thee; every man child among you shall be circumcised.
>
> And ye shall circumcise the flesh of your foreskin; and it shall be a token of the covenant betwixt me and you.
>
> And he that is eight days old shall be circumcised among you, every man child in your generations, he that is born in the house, or bought with money of any stranger, which is not of thy seed.
>
> He that is born in thy house, and he that is bought with thy money, must needs be circumcised: and my covenant shall be in your flesh for an everlasting covenant.
>
> —Genesis 17:10–13

Through this covenant, God gave Abraham a seed. This seed passes through forty-two generations and came out through the womb of a virgin called Mary and stand among us to declare; "I am the seed of Abraham," "I am the root of Jesse," "I am the lamb of God," "I am the lion of the tribe of Judah," "I am the resurrection and the life: he that believeth in me, though he were dead, yet shall he live." This seed was responsible for the final demise of the devil, praise the Lord.

After the covenant of the foreskin gave to Abraham by God, He handed over to Moses in the wilderness on the way to the Promised Land the covenant of the law. Under the covenant of the law, people were expected to keep and adhere to a set of laws in order to access their original place. The Bible says:

> And Moses came and told the people all the words of the Lord, and all the judgments: and all the people answered with one voice, and said, "All the words which the Lord hath said will we do.
> And Moses wrote all the words of the Lord, and rose up early in the morning, and built an altar under the hill, and twelve pillars, according to the twelve tribes of Israel. And he sent young men of the children of Israel, which offered burnt offerings, and peace offerings of oxen unto the Lord.
> And Moses took half of the blood, and put it in basins; and half of the blood he sprinkled on the altar.
> And he took the book of the covenant, and read in the audience of the people; and they said, "All that the Lord hath said will we do, and be obedient.
> And Moses took the blood, and sprinkled it on the people, and said, Behold the blood of the covenant, which the Lord hath made with you concerning all these words.
>
> —Exodus 24:3–8

All these were shadows of what's to come in the new covenant that our Lord Jesus sealed with His blood on the cross of Calvary.

God was still not satisfied with the performance of People under the covenant of the law because of their weakness and out of His intense love for us He ransomed His only Son as the final solution in reconciling us back to Himself.

> For God so loved the world, that he gave his only begotten
> Son, that whosoever believeth in him should not perish,
> but have everlasting life.
>
> —John 3:16

This was the final solution that took humankind back to its lost glory and fellowship with God. Jesus Christ the only begotten Son of God had to step down into our turf, lay down His life through a shameful and painful death on the cross of Calvary in order to reconcile us back to the Father.

> Therefore is there now no condemnation to them which
> are in Christ Jesus, who walk not after the flesh, but after
> the Spirit.
>
> —Romans 8:1

Friend, the moment you are in Christ, God's agenda for your life as pointed out from Genesis chapter 1 verse 26 to 30 is restored back unto you. You are taken back to your original place in the kingdom and like I said earlier, once you don't step out of this place, setback cannot locate you.

Failures and setbacks are only found in the kitty of the devil. He distribute them to people he can lay his wicked hands on either as a result of their stepping out of their original place in God or as a test of their faith in God.

Key Revelations from the Chapter

- ✓ At a point the destiny of humankind was altered
- ✓ People acted in disobedience to the Word of God through the manipulation of the devil
- ✓ The disobedience separate the divine from humanity
- ✓ The separation brought a gulf between His adoration and the mundane
- ✓ Humankind lost its original place (kingdom) and begins to toil in the abyss of deprivation
- ✓ The intensity of God's love for people could not allow God to leave them permanently in a state of hopelessness
- ✓ People were too weak to come back to God on their own
- ✓ God make a way of escape for humankind

Notes
My Learning Points

THE CONNECTING BRIDGE

A gulf was created between the natural and the supernatural following the disconnection discussed in chapter two. This brought about the need for a connecting bridge for any possible communication or interaction between them. The connecting bridge that can void the gulf between the natural and the supernatural is faith.

According to the *Oxford Advanced Learner's Dictionary*, faith is defined as trust in somebody's ability or knowledge—or trust that something will do what has been promised. This could mean trust in a friend, person, or system. This is the definition of faith as recognized by the world system. However, this is not the kind of faith we are going to be discussing in this book. We will be looking at faith as seen from the perspective of the kingdom of God: faith that connects the natural to the supernatural.

The definition of the faith that connects the natural to the supernatural is found in the book of Hebrews.

> Now faith is the substance of things hope for, the evidence of things not seen.
>
> —Hebrews 11:1

This definition gives a graphic illustration of what faith in the kingdom represents: the substance of things hoped for and the evidence of things not seen. Faith in the kingdom is having picture of things promised in the Word of God that are yet to be seen in the physical (in your spirit mind). It gives form to the hopes you have in God and wraps God's promises for you with a tangible picture in your spirit mind.

Faith is tied to hope—your hope in God and His Word. Hope establishes a definite goal to be attained. Hope energizes and propels us toward the attainment of a goal. Therefore, it is clear from the above definition of kingdom faith that only those who have hope need faith.

I want you to take note of something from the definition of faith given here. Faith is now. It is a present thing. It is not in the past. When the moment you are hoping for is delivered, you move to the next level of hope. For what you have received you don't hope for any longer. Your hope is the foundation of your faith.

Faith can also be looked at as engaging the Word of God in order to enforce the delivery of our destinies. Faith is a powerful force that carries with it creative powers beyond measure. We understand through the scripture that;

> Through faith we understand that the worlds were framed
> by the Word of God, so that things which are seen were
> not made of things which do appear.
> —Hebrews 11:3

God is the author of faith. In the scripture above, *frame* from the Greek translation means "perfect, repair, restore, and mend." Through faith, the Word of God brought about the wonders that beheld us today. This is called creation. Since we are created and made in the image and likeness of this God, we cannot function without this spiritual force called faith.

Your faith keeps you in line with God's plan and will for your life. It brings the help you need for attaining hope. There is no basis for faith if you don't have anything to hope for. Hope that you are what you are and will be what God says you will be by his grace. I'm not talking about your hope in men, which often fails. I'm talking about your hope in Elohim.

> For we are saved by hope; but hope that is seen is not hope;
> for what a man seeth, why doth he yet hope for?
>
> —Romans 8:24

This hope is given to you through the shed blood of Jesus Christ in demonstration of His divine love for you.

To qualify to be of faith, you must have a consciousness of something supernatural and absolutely believe in it. In this sense, we are talking about God and His wondrous works and promises. A man or a woman of faith in the kingdom approaches God and believes that God is a rewarder of those who diligently seek Him. Your faith in God creates a space for reward in the kingdom for you. This clearly brings to mind that there are two levels of receiving in God's kingdom.

When your faith comes alive, you immediately receive in the spiritual realm. What you received in the spiritual realm is represented by a mental picture of what you believed God would do for you. Even though those around you might not be able to feel or see what you believed God would do, you can actually see, feel, and handle your expectations in your spirit mind before the physical manifestation.

The second level of receiving with the kingdom faith is the physical manifestation of what you already have: the mental picture in your spirit mind. This level of receiving (physical manifestation) is accomplished by putting your faith to work or action.

Men and women without faith are dead spiritually. They are dead because they are disconnected from God. You can imagine what happens to a product that is disconnected from the purpose and will of its manufacturer. Such a product may exist, but it is already in the trash. It belongs in the trash bin. Without faith, all your efforts will amount to nothing.

> But without faith it is impossible to please him; for he that cometh to God must believe that He is, and is a rewarder of them that diligently seek Him."
>
> Hebrews 11:6

God is a rewarder, but He rewards only those who please and seek Him through faith. It takes faith to seek Him. Praise God for this revelation. If God is absolute—everything, I Am That I Am, and a rewarder of those who please Him through faith—what are you waiting for? Get soaked with faith in Him and see the unexplainable hand of God manifesting in your life.

Getting the breakthrough you desire in your career, business, relationship, marriage, or other areas of your life does not take all the stress and struggle. You only need to believe and trust in Him. If you desire a breakthrough, you have hope. The fact that you are holding this book right now is an indication of the hope in you. Based on this hope, it is time to connect the supernatural with your faith.

Most people prefer doing things the hard way without actually realizing it. This is why many people do not take seriously the eternal prescription and truth revealed in this book. Faith in God brings reward sounds cheap and irrational. Many people depend entirely on their experiences. What they can't understand, they don't believe. Being overtly rational means you don't leave room for the supernatural—and you are a god to yourself. King-David declares:

> The law of the Lord is perfect, converting the soul: the testimony of the Lord is sure, making wise the simple.
>
> —Psalm 19:7

I pray that God will open your eyes to this simple truth today in the mighty name of Jesus.

Beloved, let's get deeper now about this thing called faith. Faith in the kingdom is a higher dimension of trusting and believing. Believing is having trust in something and having confidence in the ability of a thing to deliver expected results as promised. In the event of a contrary result to an expectation in a believing system, the system is altered—and the trust might be lost. However, faith is that state of believing that does not depend or wait upon the outcome or physical manifestation of what is believed. Whatever wind blows, kingdom faith remains unchangeable. Many people claim *seeing is believing*. This is in direct contrast to what faith in the kingdom represents. Jesus said, "Blessed are they that have not seen and yet have believed."

> Jesus said unto him, "Thomas, because thou hast seen me, thou hast believed; blessed are they that have not seen, and yet have believed."
>
> —John 20:29

Seeing before believing is a lie from the pit of hell. This lie is holding many captive. Many are waiting today to see results before they can believe.

> Except I shall see in his hands the print of the nails and put my finger into the print of the nails, and thrust my hand into his side, I will not believe.
>
> —John 20:25

Many people say, "Show me your result, and then I will believe in what you are saying." This attitude might be right to some extent in our dealings with fellow human beings, but we should not extend the same to our relationship with our Heavenly Father. Putting up such an attitude with God demonstrates that you are faithless. The Bible says you cannot please Him without faith. The truth espoused in this book will set you free in Jesus's name.

Faith does not wait until he sees in the physical. However, it does not mean faith is blind; it actually sees in the spiritual. Faith takes God at His word and generates an image of the promise in the spirit mind. In essence, faith is not blind. It sees in the spirit mind first. To qualify as faith, your believing must get to the level that it does not wait until you see physically. Receive the promise and get a picture of the fulfilled promise in your spirit mind.

Belief can change when the outcomes of what is believed turn contrary. However, kingdom faith doesn't change irrespective of the physical outcome to what is believed; it is constant. Commanding faith is unwavering. The outcome changes nothing. You are completely sold out to what you believed because you can picture the promise of God and take hold of it in your spirit mind. You also know that His integrity is constant. Praise God. His integrity is sure, and it cannot change.

The fact that the physical manifestation did not occur when you expect it does not mean the promise failed. This is where faith lines are drawn, and it is the point where most Christians who profess faith drop it. Faith that cannot pass the point of no return is not faith; it is mere believing. Always have it at the back of your mind that even though it tarries, it will speak at the appointed time.

God is a god of timing; He knows the right time to bless you. As a perfect God, He does not engage in imperfection. He will not bring you a blessing that will introduce sorrow to your life. Everything He will do will bring glory to His name and lift you up. The time He takes to show up builds up your character and strength.

> For the vision is yet for an appointed time, but at the end it
> shall speak, and not lie; though it tarry, wait for it, because
> it will surely come, it will not tarry.
>
> —Habakkuk 2:3

When the three Hebrew boys—Shadrach, Meshach, and Abednego—were faced with the fury of king Nebuchadnezzar, they demonstrated a faith that passed mere believing. They believed God would deliver them from the hands of King Nebuchadnezzar. They boldly declared:

> If it be so, our God whom we serve is able to deliver us
> from the burning fiery furnace and He will deliver us out
> of thine hand, O king. But if not, be it known unto thee,
> O king that we will not serve thy gods, nor worship the
> golden image which thou hast set up.
>
> —Daniel 3:17–18

I love the second leg of the scripture quoted above. The boys talked boldly, loudly, and clearly to the king. They said, "We know the God we serve is able to deliver us from thy hand, but per adventure He did not, be it known to you king, that does not make Him a failed God. He remains our God and we will not worship your own god."

They refused to worship the image the king set up despite the threat to their lives. They knew very well that God was more than able to deliver them. This level of belief in God moved from just believing to faith. They drew the faith line. They made it clear to the king; irrespective of what happens to us because of your actions, we will not worship your image because our God is God. These boys knew and believed in the Word of God in exodus:

> Thou shall worship no other gods for the Lord, whose
> name is jealous, is a jealous God; before me.
>
> —Exodus 34:14

They did not give King Nebuchadnezzar the opportunity to wait and see the outcome of what they believed before proving the supremacy of God. They challenged the most powerful authority of that time with the supremacy of God through faith. Do you know God has the power to prevent the king from throwing them into the burning furnace, but He waited till they got inside the furnace to manifest His majesty? Kingdom faith compels God to act. When they landed inside the fiery furnace, God was waiting for them there.

> Then Nebuchadnezzar the king was astonished and rose
> up in haste, and spake, and said unto his counselors, "Did
> not we cast three men bound into the midst of the fire?"
> They answered and said unto the king, "True, O king." He
> answered and said, "Lo, I see four men loose, walking in
> the midst of the fire, and they have no hurt; and the form
> of the fourth is like the Son of God."
>
> —Daniel 3:24–25

Whenever you get to this level with any situation or issue, you are challenging God to His words. God is bound to perform that which is said because His words can never return to Him void.

> So shall my Word be that goes out of my mouth;
> It shall not return to Me void,
> But it shall accomplish what I please,
> And it shall prosper in the thing for which I sent it.
>
> —Isaiah 55:11

You can imagine the honor brought upon these boys by their faith in God. As your faith comes alive, I see God showing forth in that unpleasant situation in Jesus's name. Anywhere they are forcing you to bow, with your faith released; God will show forth and manifest His glory in the name of Jesus. If God had said it, He will bring it to pass in your life as long as you have faith in Him.

To meet the metric of faith, your words and actions must be in synergy with the picture in your spirit mind. Faith begins with knowing the promises of God concerning you. These promises are contained in the Word of God. The promises give rise to a mental picture in your spirit mind. You progress to confessions of faith with your mouth and demonstrate it with your actions. In other words, you must see what is possible with the Word of God. Think possibility with God and act possibility in God.

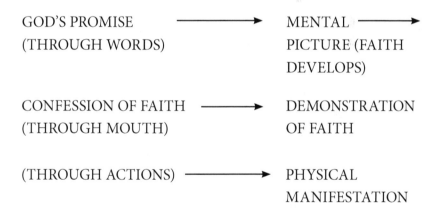

GOD'S PROMISE ⟶ MENTAL ⟶
(THROUGH WORDS)   PICTURE (FAITH
                  DEVELOPS)

CONFESSION OF FAITH ⟶ DEMONSTRATION
(THROUGH MOUTH)   OF FAITH

(THROUGH ACTIONS) ⟶ PHYSICAL
                    MANIFESTATION

The illustration depicted above explains how kingdom faith is developed and put to work. This is clearly encapsulated in Paul's letter to the Romans:

> For with the heart one believes unto righteousness, and
> with mouth confession is made unto salvation.
>
> —Romans 10:10

Faith is indispensable to living a victorious Christian life. Without it, you cannot profess to be a Christian.

> But without faith it is impossible to please him,
> For he who comes to God must believe that he is,
> And that he is a rewarder of those who diligently seek him.
>
> —Hebrews 11:6

How do you seek something you don't believe exists? How do you diligently seek something you do not have a mental picture of? What do you hinge your believe on if you don't know what it is capable of doing for you? A Christian who wants to appropriate the powers of God needs to have a mental picture of God and know what He is capable of doing. This explains why Moses asked the question at his encounter with God at the burning bush:

> Then Moses said to God "Indeed,
> When I come to the children of Israel and say to them.
> 'The God of your father has sent me to you'
> And they say to me, 'What is his name?'
> What shall I say to them?"
> And God said to Moses, "I Am Who I Am."
> And he said, "Thus you shall say to the children of Israel,
> 'I Am has sent me.'
>
> —Exodus 3:13–14

I Am Who I Am means I am everything. I will be to you whatever your spirits mind can take me to be. I am whatever your mind can conceive of me. I am whatever picture you have of me. I make it a reality to you. In whatever form you carry me, I go with you without failing.

God described himself in a powerful way. That is why God is omnipotent and omnipresent. He is the Alpha and the Omega, the first and the last, and the one who was before everything and will continue to be after all things. Hallelujah.

Whatever you believe God can do, He will do without failing. If you believe God can heal you of a sickness, He will heal you. If you believe God can take you out of a financial mess, He will take you out of it. If you believe God will come through for you in a situation, He will come through for you. Praise God.

> And the Lord said unto Abraham, "Wherefore did Sarah laugh, saying, 'Shall I of surety bear a child, which am old?' Is anything too hard for the Lord? At the time appointed I will return unto thee, according to the time of life, and Sarah shall have a son."
>
> —Genesis 18:13–14

Faith is acting in wisdom. The Bible says:

> A wise man fears and departs from evil, but a fool rages and is self-confident.
>
> —Proverb 14:16

A faithless person is a fool. I wonder how a full-blooded person would desire to be a fool. Get wise today and begin to act in faith. God deals with men and women according to the measure of the person's faith.

> For I say through the grace given to me, to every man that is among you, not to think of himself more highly than he ought to think; but to think soberly, according as God has dealt to every man the measure of faith.
>
> —Romans 12:3

There is no dealing without faith. Friend, what is your mental picture of God? Take a moment to reflect. What is your personal conviction about God? What do you think He is capable of doing for you? Your answers to these questions are your first step toward living a life of faith. Begin to see God in a position of taking you out of that challenge right now. Start to view Him from the perspective of a loving father. Just imagine what a loving father will do for his children.

I have two lovely sons, and I love them to the point where sometimes I strained myself to provide for them as a demonstration of my love. Our Heavenly Father loves and has inexhaustible resources to meet our needs. Most people only see God as someone sitting on a throne and ditching out judgment upon judgment to those who have wronged Him. No! He is a God of love. He loves us so much that—even in our sins and unrighteousness— He still ransomed His only begotten Son for us, so that we can be connected back to the glory He already prepared for us to enjoy. God is not just the Creator; He has established a father-son relationship with you through His Son Jesus Christ. He created you, and He has good intention for you.

> For I know the thoughts that I think toward you, saith the Lord, thoughts of peace, and not of evil, to give you an expected end.
>
> —Jeremiah 29:11

There is an expected end for you; the Lord said so. All you need is faith to connect with the promise.

Faith is the foundation for a glorious Christian way of living. Without it, you are in enmity with God. Being in enmity with God is acting foolishly. Wisdom brings liberation; having faith in God confirms you are wise. Faith conquers fear. It makes the impossible possible. Through it, destiny is fulfilled, weakness becomes strength, and breakdowns become breakthroughs. Failure in life is not on God's agenda for you.

> Beloved, I pray that you may prosper in all things and be
> in health just as your soul prospers.
>
> —3 John 1:2

God has a glorious destination for you, and it takes faith to get there. Faith is the means of exchange in the supernatural. You use faith to get what you desire from God. Your numerous needs are met by God's inexhaustible supply through the currency of faith. The more of it you have, the more transactions you can carry out with God. Money is the means of exchange in the world, but faith is the means of exchange in the spiritual realm.

> Behold the proud,
> His soul is not upright in him;
> But the just shall live by his faith
>
> —Habakkuk 2:4

There is no living without faith. Some Christians are suffering from faith poverty. They are born again quite well but are low in faith. They have little or nothing in their faith accounts to transact with the supernatural. Faith as a means of exchange in the supernatural makes it expendable. As you use up your faith, you must ensure that it is replenished. As we fellowship and share the Word of God with other brethren in the Lord, our faith is replenished and built up.

Having no faith at all is a worst-case scenario. If you are faithless, you are dead to the supernatural. When you enter a supermarket, meeting your shopping needs depends on two things: how much money you can afford to spend and whether what you need is in stock or out of stock. You may have money (means of transaction), but what you need is out of stock. This is not so with God. As long as your faith—the currency to transact with the supernatural—is in place, your needs can never be out of stock in God's supplies. In fact, His supplies are inexhaustible. Understanding this truth will launch you into a lack-free life. Apostle Paul gave us this assurance in the Lord;

> And my God will supply all your need according to his riches in glory by Christ Jesus.
> —Philippians 4:19

Jehovah said, "I will supply all your needs." What are you waiting for? Take hold of this promise, launch out with your faith, and begin to appropriate the inexhaustible supply of your Father in heaven. These things are there for you, and it is your redemptive right to appropriate them. However, you need the currency to transact with heaven—and that is your faith.

Faith also represents the bridge that connects the natural and the supernatural. Bridges serve as link between two points. When a gulf exists between two points, you need a bridge to cross between the points. A gulf exists between the natural and the supernatural, and you need the faith bridge to cross from the natural to the supernatural.

The supernatural is where power and authority is found. It is where you take hold of your destiny. If you are satisfied with where you are and have no desire to explore the other side, there is no need for a bridge. But the moment you desire to connect with the other side, the need for a bridge becomes imperative. If you desire a change in your present condition, you need a *faith bridge* to connect with the supernatural.

Everything that happens in the natural is predetermined in the supernatural. In order to not to be a gambler in the natural, you need to connect to the supernatural with the faith bridge and get involved in the proper shaping of your natural. Your natural represents the physical manifestation of your destiny.

The natural is determined in the supernatural. If you are not satisfied with your current situation—or the situation is not in conformity with the Word of God—launch out with your faith. Changes will come. Get involved in the shaping of your natural in the supernatural.

Friend, there are treasures in the deep. It takes launching into the deep to experience a net-breaking catch. These treasures cannot be accessed through toiling. They can only be accessed through faith. I command you to come out of your toiling now in Jesus's mighty name.

Simon was delivered from toiling when he connected to the supernatural with his faith on the Lord's command.

> Now when He had left speaking, He said unto Simon, "Launch out into the deep, and let down your nets for a draught." And Simon answering said unto him, "Master, we have toiled all the night, and have taken nothing: nevertheless at thy word, I will let down the net." And when they had this done, they enclosed a great multitude of fishes; and their net brake.
>
> —Luke 5:4–6

Net-breaking miracles take place whenever faith is exercised. Jesus told Simon to release his faith (the net) even under the condition that had not worked for him in the past. Human efforts and abilities without faith in God amount to nothing. Simply put, it amounts to toiling. With all the experience of Simon and his fishing colleagues, they toiled all night without a catch. They went fishing at the most appropriate time to catch fish—at night—but they toiled all night without catching any. The moment they connected with the supernatural through faith, the maker of all fishes gave them a draught in the same place they had being toiling.

Where you are might not be the problem. Your current job might not be the problem. The people around you aren't responsible for your unpleasant situation. Have you connected the supernatural and your faith? God's grace abounds to help you in that difficult situation, but he is waiting to see your faith released. Faith plus grace equals abundance. Effort minus faith equals toiling. Receive your own abundance now in the name of Jesus.

Key Revelations from the Chapter

- ✓ There is the need for the natural to connect with the supernatural.
- ✓ The connecting bridge between the natural and the supernatural is the faith bridge.
- ✓ Faith believes God and the Word of God.
- ✓ Faith is a force, and it has creative power.
- ✓ We can only function by faith.
- ✓ Receiving from the supernatural requires faith.
- ✓ Faith is seeing with the mind's eye.
- ✓ Faith is unwavering, and it does not change with the outcome of our expectation.
- ✓ It is the currency in the kingdom of God.
- ✓ Faith is the means of exchange in the supernatural.

Notes
My Learning Points

Developing or Building
the Bridge

If faith has been identified as the connecting bridge to the supernatural and the preceding chapter defined what faith in the kingdom represents—and what it can do for you—other important questions will agitate your mind: How do I develop this faith? How do I build this important bridge? What can I do to live in faith? This chapter will provide you with the insight to answer these questions.

Faith is developed. It is not something you are born with. It can't be bought at the supermarket. It comes to you through your conscious efforts to receive it.

> So then faith comes by hearing, and hearing by the Word of God.
>
> —Romans 10:17

Apostle Paul admonished the Romans and gave the recipe for developing faith. It comes through hearing of the Word of God. You don't pray for faith or ask for faith; it comes to you through hearing the Word of God. To develop kingdom faith, you have to make yourself available to hearing the Word of God and understanding it. The Word of God is a seed. It carries the ability to germinate in your heart and brings forth godly fruits in your life, including faith. In other words, faith is a fruit produced through the planting, nurturing, and bringing forth of the Word of God in your heart. The Word of God is his sovereignty; it is His might and power. He can do nothing without the Word of God. The Bible says:

> In the beginning was the Word, and the Word was with God, and the Word was God. The same was in the beginning with God. All things were made by him; and without him was not anything made that was made
>
> —John 1: 1–3

The Word of God conveys His mind toward us, reveals His love for us, and brings to our knowledge the heritage we have in Him. It takes knowing and understanding the Word of God to be able to come to terms with who God is to you. This can only happen by availing yourself the opportunity of hearing the Word of God.

We learned that every miracle from God is preceded by the release of our faith. Therefore, it is important for us to cultivate the habit of constantly sitting at the feet of the Holy Spirit to feed on the Word of God and develop faith in Him. You have to locate a Bible-believing church and sit under the anointing to constantly hear the Word of God. It takes feeding on the Word of God for faith to come alive. What you listen to feeds your mind. The words we listen to feed our minds and affect our well-being in the same way what we eat affects our muscles and growth.

> Take heed therefore unto yourselves and to all the flock, over the which the Holy Ghost hath made you overseers, to feed the church of God, which he hath purchased with his own blood.
>
> —Acts 20:28

Whatever has dominance over your thoughts determines your belief system and builds your faith. Just as natural food brings about the development of our bodies, so too does the Word of God develop our faith. If you eat bad food, you will either be plagued by diseases or have stunted growth. The same applies with what you feed your mind. If you give your mind to the perverse things of the world—especially the lies from the pit of hell—your heart will bring forth fruits of fear rather than faith, which is needed to please God. Don't forget that the words we listen to are seeds that are sown in our minds. They germinate and bring forth fruits in our lives. Your mind is always a ready ground to receive the Word of God as seeds and bring them to fruit-bearing plants. These fruits are expressed through faith or fear.

If a seed is preserved, it will always retain its potential to germinate and bring forth fruits when planted on a fertile soil. The moment a well preserved seed gets on a good soil, it will blossom and radiate its potential. The Word of God is preserved in the scriptures. They carry the potential to turn around any situation and perform whatever they have been sent forth to do. They are waiting to find the fertile soil in our minds to reach their potential. These expressions depend upon how the soil of our hearts receives them. If your heart is not polluted or full of weeds from the lies of the devil, the seed will take root and bring forth good fruits. If your heart is polluted and overgrown with weeds and thorns—or is patched with lies from hell—the seed of the Word of God cannot achieve its potential. In such cases, you will need to remove every undesirable weed or thorn in your heart through repentance and grace from the shed blood of Jesus Christ.

Jesus used the parable of the sower to teach us on the importance of the condition of our heart in receiving the Word of God. In the parable, he discussed different kinds of soil (hearts a seed can fall upon).

A sower went out to sow his seed,

And as he sowed, some fell by the wayside; and it was trampled down,

And the birds of the air devoured it

Some fell on the rock; and as soon as it sprang up, it withered away because it lacked moisture.

And some fell among thorns, and the thorns sprang up with it and choked it

But others fell on good ground,

Sprang up, and yielded a crop a hundredfold.

—Luke 8:5–8

Jesus didn't stop at speaking in parables this time. He took time to explain the parable to His disciples.

Now the parable is this;

The seed is the Word of God.

Those by the way side are they that hear; then cometh the devil, and taketh away the Word out of their hearts; lest they should believe and be saved.

They on the rock are they, which, when they hear, receive the Word with joy; and these have no root which for a while believe, and in time of temptation fall away.

And that which fell among thorns are they, which, when they have heard, go forth, and are choked with cares and riches and pleasure of this life, and bring no fruit to perfection.

But those on the good ground are they, which in an honest and good heart, having heard the Word, keep it, and bring forth fruit with patience.

—Luke 8:11–15

The most important words for the fruitfulness of the Word of God in our hearts are keeping it with patience. What you hear determines what you see, and what you see will always shape what you become.

> Verily, verily, I say unto you, the hour is coming and now
> is when the dead shall hear the voice of the Son of God:
> and they that hear shall live.
>
> —John 5:25

Our eyes and ears are the two gateway into our mind. You keep the dominant words you hear. If the Word of God is what you are exposed to most of the time, it dominates your heart and brings forth faith in God. If you allow the lies from the pit of hell to dominate what you listen to, it will choke the few words of God that have found their ways into your heart and will produce the fruit of fear. You also need to keep the Word of God in your heart and exercise your faith with patience. Remember that He promised, and He is able to bring to pass what He promised.

Check out how receptive your heart is to the Word of God. Is it stony or fleshy? Faith cannot develop if you carry a stony heart. The words are coming, and satan is picking them up before they get the chance to germinate. This happens mostly with critical people. Critical people question everything they hear. They are overly rational. Watch out! People with such hearts rarely develop faith.

Be careful. When you have been walked on and disappointed, you can become callous. Your heart can develop an impenetrable shield that choke the seed of the Word of God with negative life experiences.

Faith only comes by continually hearing the Word of God. I want you to keep something in the back of your mind: satan is not interested in anything you have other than your faith. He attacks your blessings, including your health, so that you can lose your faith and throw up your hands in defeat. Remember what he did to Job.

Job had a relationship with God because he believed in Him. In return, God blessed him to the point that God can boast of Job's righteousness (his faith) to His archenemy.

> And the Lord said unto satan, "Hast thou considered my servant Job, that there is none like him in the earth, a perfect and an upright man, one that feareth God and eschweth evil?"
> Then satan answered the Lord, and said, "Doth Job fear God for naught? Hast not thou made a hedge about him, and about his house, and about all that he hath on every side? Thou hast blessed the work of his hands, and his substance is increased in the land. But put forth thine hand now and touch all that he hath and he will curse thee to thy face."
>
> —Job 1:8–11

From the scripture quoted above, it can be inferred that the target of satan in Job's life is his faith. His utmost desire is to see Job lose his faith in God and curse God to His face. To achieve his plan for Job, satan employed the strategy of attacking Job's possessions, health, and well-being to the point that he would lose his faith and curse God. In other words, satan was trying to destroy Job's faith. Satan wanted Job to lose his faith in God and renounce God's lordship over him.

The target of satan attack in the life of any believer is faith—not his possessions or blessings. The moment you know this and guide your faith jealously, the devil has lost the battle. The devil is not attacking your job because he needs one. He is not coming after your blessing because he needs to give it to another person. The devil doesn't bless people, including his agents and principalities. The devil wants to break the relationship that exists between you and your Heavenly Father through faith. Don't forget the devil knows the scripture too. Remember his encounter with Jesus in the wilderness after Jesus fasted for forty days and forty nights.

> And saith unto him, if thou be the Son of God, cast thyself down: for it is written, he shall give his angels charge concerning thee; and in their hands they shall bear thee up, least at any time thou dash thy foot against a stone.
>
> —Matthew 4:6

Satan knew for sure that you cannot please God without faith, and he wanted you to be in enmity with your Creator. That is his number one assignment on earth. I have good news for you. No matter how fierce the battle is, there will always be a recovery. Don't lose your faith. Despite his troubles, Job demonstrated an unwavering faith in God. What happened to Job afterward? Restoration! Hallelujah.

> So the Lord blessed the latter end of Job more than his beginning: for he had fourteen thousand sheep, and six thousand camels, and a thousand yoke of oxen and a thousand she asses.
>
> —Job 42:12

Moreover, the scripture encourages us not to faint in our faith in God. Reaping will come from our steadfastness.

> And let us not be weary in well doing, for in due season we shall reap, if we faint not.
>
> —Galatians 6:9

Well doing means pleasing God through faith, and if you faint not by not losing your faith, then your reaping is certain in God's appointed time. Our faith is the target of the devil;

> And the Lord said, "Simon, behold, satan hath desired to
> have you, that he may sift you as wheat: But I have prayed
> for thee, that thy faith fail not."
> —Luke 22:31–32

Jesus is saying, "I won't stop satan from desiring to have you, but I have interceded on your behalf that in those trying periods, you will not lose your faith."

Friend, guide your faith with diligence. It is the only treasure you have that the devil is eyeing. The devil is mad that you have faith in God, and he is ready to go to any length to see you lose the faith. My prayer for you this day is that your faith will not fail in Jesus's name.

Another thing that determines your living in faith is your root system. What is your root system? Are you rooted in God or you have no iota of relationship with Him? Your root system determines your level of faith. Therefore, you need to be careful because we live in a world of shallow relationships, superficial conversations, and hurried moments of prayer. We bounce from one spiritual activity to another without any root system. Get real with yourself, do a soil analysis of your heart, and weed out anything that's hindering your developing faith. Once your heart is tender and receptive, your devotion is deep, and your life is uncluttered, you'll be a good ground for great faith to develop and yield fruits for God.

The heart is the seat of faith; it is the well from which faith flows. Whatever is in your heart determines what your mouth says. What you say shapes your actions, and your actions produce results in your life. King Solomon captured this in one of his proverbs:

> Keep thy heart with all diligence; for out of it are the issues
> of life.
>
> —Proverbs 4:23

If you allow the Word of God to permeate your heart, it grows into a mighty plant of faith. If you allow the lies of the devil to fill your heart, it produces fruits of fear, intimidation, and failure. Make conscious efforts to fill your heart with the Word of God so that words of faith will come out of your mouth.

Here is a simple test to check if you are living in faith or not. Check what is coming out of your mouth. If what is coming out of your mouth is not in conformity with the Word of God, you should know that your heart is filled with lies from hell.

> Brood of vipers! How can you, being evil, speak good
> things? For out of the abundance of the heart the mouth
> speaks.
>
> —Matthew 12:34

Your faith also comes alive via the company you keep. If you walk in the company of fools, you will exhibit foolishness. Your faith commands blessings upon your life, and it takes your walk in the counsel of the godly for you to be blessed.

> Blessed is the man who walks not in the counsel of the
> ungodly,
> Nor stands in the path of sinners,
> Nor sits in the seat of the scornful;
> But his delight is in the law of the Lord
> And in his law he meditates day and night.

And he shall be like a tree planted by the rivers of waters;
that bring forth his fruit in his season; his leaf also shall
not wither; and whatsoever he doeth shall prosper.

—Psalm 1:1–3

Friends, you have to be conscious of this fact. Associate only with people who will help your faith. Your blessing is guaranteed in your walking in the counsel of such people. When you associate with people of no faith, people who do not know their heritage in our Lord Jesus Christ, and the lost ones in this glorious generation, you are bound to fail in your efforts to develop a winning faith.

Choose your friends, choose the company you keep, and discern the counsel you listen to because they go a long way in determining how far you get along in developing faith. People say, "Show me your friends, and I will tell you who you are." The Bible have this to say;

Iron sharpeneth iron; so a man sharpeneth the countenance
of his friend.

—Proverbs 27:17

The company you keep is very important in your faith walk with God. Be careful in choosing your friends, and stop jumping into relationships with people you don't know, especially if you don't have any idea about their relationship with God. Many are in the cage of the devil today because of the relationships they keep.

Sometimes we make mistakes, but we usually allow ourselves to plunge into the sea of sin because of the relationship we keep. Take steps to be in charge of your decision-making process today, especially as it relates to the company you keep. Move with people who fear God and see you on the side of victory.

Key Revelations from the Chapter

- ✓ Faith is developed through conscious efforts.
- ✓ It comes through hearing and understanding of the Word of God.
- ✓ Faith is rooted in the heart.
- ✓ We feed our minds with what we listen and pay attention to.
- ✓ Faith flourishes by keeping the Word of God in our hearts and having patience.
- ✓ Satan's number one assignment on earth is attacking the faith of believers.
- ✓ What is coming out of your mouth will indicate if you are a person of faith or not.
- ✓ Your faith life is influenced by the company you keep.

Notes
My Learning Points

Levels and Types of Bridges

Drawing from the analogy of the natural bridge, you will agree with me that there are different types of bridges. We have rope bridges, plank bridges, and rock-solid bridges that are built to withstand pressures and loads. You will also agree that the weight these bridges can carry will depend upon their type and strength. However, no matter the type of bridge, it will still deliver that which it is meant to deliver by connecting two points. In the same vein, faiths are in different levels just as bridges are in different shapes and sizes.

As was pointed out earlier, faith is the currency in the economy of the kingdom. You transact with it. The level of your faith is determined by the amount of the Word of God you've heard, understood, and allowed to be profitable in your life. The one you kept and acted on with patience. If faith comes from hearing the Word of God, it means how much of the Word of God you hear determines the level of your faith. Please don't get me wrong at this point. I'm talking about the Word of God that you heard that found a good soil in your heart that allows it to germinate and bring forth fruits. I'm not talking about the words you heard that could not find appropriate soil in your heart to germinate, much less bring forth fruits.

However, irrespective of the level of your faith, it produces tangible results in your hand like the analogy of the natural bridge I drew above. Jesus was teaching on the subject of faith on a particular day, and He pointed out to His disciples that exercising faith as little as a mustard seed will produce great results.

> So Jesus said to them, "Because of your unbelief, for assuredly, I say to you, if you have faith as a mustard seed, you will say to this mountain, move from here to there, and it will move; and nothing will be impossible for you."
>
> —Matthew 17:20

A mustard seed is one of the smallest seeds you can come across. Jesus was teaching His disciples that they should do away with unbelief in their hearts and allow faith—no matter how little—to permeate their hearts. It is only then that they can do great works, and nothing shall be impossible for them. Faith, as little as the mustard seed, is very potent. It can move mountains.

You don't need to wait until you are able to develop great faith before exercising it. Start exercising faith in little things, and God will prove His faithfulness to you. Your faith level will grow. Don't despise your faith when it is at the little level because it will produce great proof if you put it to work.

However, strive not to remain at a low level of faith forever. Life is about growth and making progress. The more God is manifesting and revealing your purpose to you and the world, the more the opposition you will see from the devil. Our adversaries are always on duty and resisting us. We can only overcome the devil with our faith.

> Who is he that overcometh the world, but he that believeth that Jesus is the Son of God?
>
> —1 John 5:5

The scripture emphasizes the need for growth. You can't afford to remain a child in the kingdom forever. The inheritance packaged for you the moment you were born again can only be released for your total control when you grow in the kingdom.

> Now I say, "That the heir, as long as he is a child, differeth
> nothing from a servant, though he be lord of all;
> But is under tutors and governors until the time appointed
> of the Father.
> Even so we, when we were children, were in bondage under
> the elements of the world."
> —Galatians 4:1–3

Don't get scared. It does not matter the level of faith you are operating in now; what is important is being a person of faith. As you continue to exercise it, it develops more and more. Nothing stops you from becoming a faith giant like our father Abraham. The Bible says he hoped against hope. What a great faith!

Going further on this, faith can be categorized into three levels. These include the no faith level, little faith level, and great faith level. Your level of faith determines the result it delivers to you.

No Faith Level

The most dangerous faith level to operate in is the no faith level. If you are operating at this level, it means you are not connected with the supernatural. You are completely operating in the flesh, which is the natural. You are a god unto yourself, and the unfortunate thing is that you can't survive the battles the enemies will bring your way when operating in the natural.

Life situations only answer to those who are operating in the supernatural. When the disciples of Jesus were confronted with the storm, they were perishing because they were operating at the no faith level.

And there arose a great storm of wind, and the waves beat
into the ship, so that it was now full.

And he was in the hinder part of the ship, asleep on a
pillow: and they awake him, and say unto him, "Master,
carest thou not that we perish?"

And he arose, and rebuked the wind, and said unto the
sea, "Peace, be still." And the wind ceased, and there was
a great calm.

And he said unto them, "Why are ye so fearful? How is it
that ye have no faith?"

—Mark 4:37–40

Even with God's presence around you, if you are operating at no
faith level, you are a sure candidate for the devil's harassments
and intimidations. Despite the fact that Jesus was in the boat with
them, they were still being harassed by the storm because they were
operating at no faith level.

At the no faith level, the spirit of fear is in control. This is because
life gives no room for vacuum. It is either your life is filled with the
Holy Spirit or that of the devil. There is no sitting on the fence. The
spirit of fear is not of God—it is from the devil.

For God hath not given us the spirit of fear; but of power,
and of love, and of sound mind.

—2 Timothy 1:7

Operating at no faith level indicates that you have a reprobate mind
instead of a sound mind. Friend, you need to bring yourself out of
this level. It is too dangerous for you to stay in.

Little Faith or Small Faith Level

The next level of faith after the no faith level is the little faith or small faith level. This is the first level of faith any believer can operate in. However, there is a big difference between this level and the no faith level. Here you are actually connected with and operating in the supernatural.

With this faith level, you can tell a mountain to be removed and cast into yonder—and it will obey you. The moment you believe with your heart and confess with your mouth that Jesus Christ is Lord and that He died to save you, faith is already in place. The grace present in the redemptive blood of the lamb is made available to you, and you are above principalities and powers. Every-born again child of God has a measure of faith.

> For I say, through the grace given unto me, to every man
> that is among you, not to think of himself more highly
> than he ought to think; but to think soberly, according as
> God hath dealt to every man the measure of faith.
>
> —Romans 12:3

As a believer, God has given you a measure of faith to operate with, but it is your responsibility to add to your faith through growth. Faith is a spiritual force, and it is being constantly expended. Therefore, you cannot afford to stay at the little faith level for too long because you will run out of power.

Little faith commands little result. The results of this level of faith are at the mercy of the wind blowing your life. The moment the wind becomes boisterous, little faith will fail. Peter once operated at this faith level.

But when he saw the wind boisterous, he was afraid; and
beginning to sink, he cried, saying, "Lord save me."

And immediately Jesus stretched forth his hand, and
caught him, and said unto him, "O thou of little faith,
wherefore didst thou doubt?"

—Matthew 14:30–31

Peter was able to walk on the water because he believed Jesus when
He told him to come. Peter had faith, but since his faith was little, it
failed him the moment he saw the wind become boisterous.

Friend, you need to do an assessment of your faith level to ensure
that you move from little faith to great faith. The more you progress in
life, the more adversity you will need to confront. Since we transact in
the kingdom with faith, your level of faith determines your purchasing
power in the supernatural. Your faith level determines your strength
in the supernatural. You need strength to fight your battle, and your
strength comes from your faith.

Above all, taking the shield of faith, wherewith ye shall be
able to quench all the fiery darts of the wicked.

—Ephesians 6:16

If you have to achieve greatness in life as your Heavenly Father has
purposed for you, you have to grow from little faith to great faith.
That is the level champions operate in.

Great Faith Level

Great faith level is the level of faith in which the high fliers in the
kingdom operate. At this level of faith, you command the kingdom
of darkness—and they obey without contest. Supernatural results
are delivered to your hand without sweat. You have a voice, and even

the host of hell recognizes you as such. Apostle Paul was operating at this level of faith. Even demons and principalities recognized him and accorded him the necessary respect.

> And the evil spirit answered and said, Jesus I know, and Paul I know; but who are ye?
> —Acts 19:15

We also know of the centurion in the Bible who got a speedy miracle because of his great faith level.

> And when Jesus was entered into Capernaum, there came unto him a centurion, beseeching him,
> And saying, "Lord, my servant lieth at home sick of the palsy, grievously tormented."
> And Jesus saith unto him, "I will come and heal him."
> The centurion answered and said, "Lord, I am not worth that thou shouldest come under my roof; but speak the Word only, and my servant shall be healed.
> For I am a man under authority, having soldiers under me: and I say to this man, Go, and he goeth; and to another, Come, and he cometh; and to my servant, Do this, and he doeth it."
> When Jesus heard it, he marveled, and said to them that followed, "Verily I say unto you, I have not found so great faith, no, not in Israel."
> —Matthew 8:5–10

Jesus wanted this man to wait until He was ready to go with him to his house and heal his servant. But because of his understanding of the power in the spoken Word of the Lord, this gave him a strong faith. The servant was healed the same hour.

The same can be said of the woman with the issue of blood. Her level of faith does not need to wait to get Jesus's attention before contacting her miracle. She said, "Only if I can touch the hem of His garment shall I be made whole." She worked out her faith by pressing through the crowd and touching the hem of Jesus's garment, and the flow of blood ceased. What about the Canaanite woman? By religious arrangement, she was not qualified for a miracle from Jesus. However, her level of faith gave her what she wanted.

> But he answered and said, "I am not sent but unto the lost sheep of the house of Israel."
> Then came she and worshiped him, saying, "Lord, help me."
> But he answered and said, "It is not meet to take the children's bread, and to cast it to dogs."
> And she said, "Truth, Lord: yet the dogs eat of the crumbs which fall from their master's table."
> Then Jesus answered and said unto her, "O woman, great is thy faith: be it unto thee even as thou wilt. And her daughter was made whole from that very hour."
> —Matthew 15:24–28

Great faith opens doors all the time. It delivers without fail. If you are struggling with anything in your life, you might need to increase your level of faith. There are issues that answer only to great faith level. God is not a respecter of person, but he respects faith.

We all desire to grow in every area of life. We desire to grow in our careers, statuses, blessings, etc. Why don't we desire to grow in our spiritual lives, including our faith levels? Growth is essential; when we stop growing, we start to die.

Faith comes through hearing and hearing the Word of God. If you want to increase or move up in your faith level, all you need to do is absorb yourself in the Word of God. Take the Word, eat it, and digest it—and it will bless your soul. Prophet Jeremiah declares:

> Thy words were found, and I did eat them; and thy Word was unto me the joy and rejoicing of mine heart: for I am called by thy name, O Lord God of hosts.
>
> —Jeremiah 15:16

By the time you are filled with the Word of God, great faith will develop in you. You will be operating as a champion. Change your story today. Challenge the demon that is holding you captive by stepping up the level of faith you are operating in.

Key Revelations from the Chapter

- ✓ Faiths are in different levels.
- ✓ Your faith level is determined by the amount of the Word of God you've heard, understood, and allowed to be profitable in your life.
- ✓ No matter what level of faith you operate in, it delivers tangible results for you.
- ✓ You don't need to wait until you develop great faith to exert your faith.
- ✓ Exerting your faith—no matter how little—will cause it to develop more and more.

Notes
My Learning Points

WALKING THE BRIDGE

No matter how good or strong a bridge is, it still needs to be walked for it to deliver the result for which it was built. The need for a bridge arose because of the desire to close the gap between two points. It is recognized that something beneficial is available on the other side.

The benefits are so desirable, but the only way to access them is to get to that side. If you have realized this need and you construct a bridge across the divide to connect both points. The benefits on the other side are now accessible because of the bridge. However, the benefits will remain untapped or elusive if you refuse—or fail—to walk across the bridge. Even though the possibility of getting to the other side exists, you still have to walk across the bridge. Achieving your desire of getting to the other side will remain a mirage if you don't walk across the bridge.

Since faith is the bridge you need to connect with the supernatural—and you already have developed faith by hearing of the Word of God—you still have to walk it to produce for you. Your faith needs to be worked. Without putting it to work, the scripture says it is dead.

> Even so faith, if it hath not works, is dead, being alone.
> Yea, a man may say, "Thou hast faith, and I have works: shew me thy faith without thy works, and I will shew thee my faith by my works."

Thou believest that there is one God; thou doest well: the
devils also believe, and tremble.
But wilt thou know, O vain man, that faith without works
is dead?

—James 2:17–20

Working your faith is not a complicated process—just as walking
a bridge is as simple as A, B, C. All you need to do is make sure
your beliefs, confessions, and actions are in harmony. Make sure
that what you believe, say, and do are in total agreement. Don't
believe one thing, confess another, and do something else. The three
elements that make the working of faith must be synchronized at
all times.

Look at specific demonstrations of faith in Biblical times and
the significant result recorded with each step of faith. Examples of
men and women who walked in faith and commanded significant
proofs abound in the scripture. I want to make it clear here that the
Bible is written by the inspiration of the Holy Spirit. It recorded what
happened in the course of time in people's relationships with God.
It is not just a documentary of past events; it is a living testimony to
the awesome power of the Almighty God. The revelations contained
in such testimonies help us see God from the array of His majestic,
divine, and unchangeable nature. Hallelujah.

Let us look at five personalities in the scripture whose faith walks
changed the course of their destinies, and draw from these sources
in building our faith and putting it to work. What I have here is not
exhaustive. These may not be best accounts of faith in the scripture.
However, with the help of the Holy Spirit, I believe there is something
God wants to strengthen you with from their story.

Abel

> By faith Abel offered unto God a more excellent sacrifice
> than Cain, by which he obtained witness that he was
> righteous, God testifying of his gifts; and by it he being
> dead yet speaketh.
>
> —Hebrews 11:4

If you examine this testimony from where the account was first
recorded in Genesis 4:3–5, Cain and Abel were siblings with the
same father and mother (Adam and Eve). For the first time after the
fall of humankind in the Garden of Eden, people pursued God in
worship and brought sacrifices and offerings to God. However, there
was a distinction between the offering Abel brought before God and
that brought by Cain.

The Bible says God has respect for Abel's offering, but He has
no respect for Cain's offering. Both brought offerings from the
abundance of the blessings God gave them in the work of their hands.
Abel's offering was accepted because it was done in faith. If faith
means hearing the Word of God (Romans 10:17), then it means Abel
heard God and believed in the instructions God gave him for how to
bring his offering to God.

Cain probably did not follow God's instructions because he
couldn't believe in it. Alternatively, he believed but refused to work
out his belief and ended up having his offering rejected by God. Abel
worked his faith by bringing God an offering as commanded by God,
and this made a way for his offering to be accepted. This clearly shows
that whatever we have to offer to God—in service or substance—must
be based on our faith in His Word. Otherwise, it will amount to only
aggrandizement of flesh, and God will not respect it.

Abraham

Abraham is generally described as the father of faith.

> Therefore it is of faith, that it might be by grace; to the end
> the promise might be sure to all the seed; not to that only
> which is of the law, but to that also which is of the faith of
> Abraham, who is the father of us all,
> (As it is written, I have made thee a father of many nations)
> before him whom he believed, even God, who quickeneth
> the dead, and calleth those things which be not as though
> they were.
> Who against hope believed in hope, that he might become
> the father of many nations, according to that which was
> spoken, so shall thy seed be.
> And being not weak in faith, he considered not his own
> body now dead, when he was about an hundred years old,
> neither yet the deadness of Sarah's womb.
> He staggered not at the promise of God through unbelief;
> but was strong in faith, giving glory to God;
> And being fully persuaded, that what he has promised, he
> was able also to perform.
>
> —Romans 4:16–21

God instructed Abraham to leave his country, kindred, and father's house, and to go to a land that He (God) would show to him. Without hesitation, Abraham obeyed and left his country as instructed by God. He was seventy-five years old when he got the call, and he left with his wife. Abraham had no child at that time because Sarai was barren.

Along the line, God made a covenant with Abraham and promised to make him the father of many nations. This promise was in contrast to Abraham's condition of childlessness and the deadness of Sarai's womb, but Abraham believed God. It is important to take note that when God gave Abraham the promise, he has no children. By natural law, he and his wife had already passed childbearing age. However, Abraham believed and had faith in God.

Twenty-five years down the line, the promise was yet to be fulfilled. Abraham was not weak in faith, and he did not stagger at the promise of God.

When God eventually gave him Isaac (the promised child), Abraham demonstrated his faith in God further by giving up Isaac as an offering on the altar to the Lord as he was commanded. He worked his faith by offering Isaac up to God because he knew God who has promised is able to fulfill the promise.

> Was not Abraham our father justified by works, when he had offered Isaac his son upon the altar?
>
> —James 2:21

Today through faith, even the Gentiles are counted as Abraham's seed. He became the father of many nations. Praise God. Through faith, whatever seems impossible in the natural is very possible with God.

> But Jesus beheld them, and said unto them, with men this is impossible; but with God all things are possible.
>
> —Matthew 19:26

It does not matter what the natural is presenting to you. By using faith to connect with the supernatural, you will see the finger of God manifesting in your life in the name of Jesus.

The Woman with the Issue of Blood

The Bible recorded a woman, whose name was not even mentioned, but her exercise of faith gave her reprieve from her terrible condition, and it gave her a place to be recorded in the scripture. The Bible says this woman was plagued with blood flowing ceaselessly from her body for twelve years. Her condition had become pathetic, and she spent all her money on physicians without getting healed.

Her condition was so miserable that she couldn't hold back any of her resources to get help, but none came. She heard that Jesus, the greatest physician, was passing through the neighborhood. She did not have an appointment or any other prior contact with him. However, based on what she had heard of Jesus, she developed faith in her heart that if she could touch the hem of His garment, she would be made whole. She worked on her faith by overcoming all odds to touch the hem of His garment. Her faith brought her healing. Praise God.

No matter how hopeless your situation appears, how long it has stayed, or how much you have lost trying to fix it without luck, put to work your faith in God. Bring the issue to Jesus He will not turn you back or demand an appointment from you. He looks out for your faith, and when He sees one, your case is settled.

> And, behold, a woman which was diseased with an issue
> of blood twelve years, came behind him, and touched the
> hem of his garment;
> For she said within herself, if I may but touch his garment,
> I shall be whole.
> But Jesus turned him about, and when he saw her, he said,
> "Daughter, be of good comfort; thy faith hath made thee
> whole." And the woman was made whole from that hour.
> —Matthew 9:20–22

The Blind Man on the Way to Jericho

> And Jesus said to him, receive thy sight; thy faith hath
> saved thee.
> And immediately he received his sight, and followed him,
> glorifying God; and all the people, when they saw it, gave
> praise unto God.
>
> —Luke 18:42–43

This is a very interesting testimony of a blind beggar on the road to Jericho. The scripture took account of this man even though his name was not important enough to be mentioned. His demonstration of faith earned him an uncommon miracle that qualified him to be recorded in the Book of Life.

He was begging for alms. Since he was blind, there was no way he could see Jesus approaching him. He couldn't size Jesus up in order to seek His help. The moment he heard the multitude pass by and heard what it meant, his faith came alive. Something in him gave him an understanding that there should be solution with this man that the multitude was following.

He cried out to Jesus with faith for help, and he got his healing.

The Man at Lystra

The scripture recorded this great healing that took place on the heel of the faith of the man at Lystra. Paul and another apostle took the message of salvation to the Gentiles. While in the city of Lystra, they saw a person who had never walked in his life. The cripple steadfastly beheld Paul as he spoke the Word of God, thereby developing faith in his heart. Paul, perceiving faith in the cripple, commanded him to arise and walk. Instantly, the crippled man arose.

And there they preach the gospel.

And there sat a certain man at Lystra, impotent in his feet, being a cripple from his mother's womb, who never had walked;

The same heard Paul speak; who steadfastly beholding him, and perceiving that he had faith to be healed,

Said with a loud voice "Stand upright on thy feet." And he leaped and walked.

—Acts 14:7–10

Friends, God is not waiting to see the title you are wearing in the church before reaching out to you. God is waiting to see your faith.

There are great exploits of faith today. The miraculous is happening everywhere through the supernatural. Signs and wonders are following those who believe today. Beloved, what are you waiting for? Your miracle is next in line. Connect with the supernatural through your faith, and heaven will deliver your package into your hands. Don't pass through this world unnoticed, unsung, and uneventful. Your destiny is glorious. There is a purpose for your coming. The whole world is waiting for your manifestation. Don't rob yourself of your place in destiny. Get connected today, and your story will change permanently in Jesus's name.

Friend, stop holding yourself down. Many people are connecting with the supernatural and receiving great blessings with their faith. It is time you are counted among the faithful believers. Break loose from that bondage—and let your faith come alive. Your breakthrough is at the mercy of your faith. I break every yoke that is holding your faith bound today in the name of Jesus. You just have to drop your cynical attitude. The End Time Church is imbued with power from high above, and they are followed with signs and wonders. When you see people trooping to the House of God, don't consider it a fluke. In fact, it is the fulfillment of the prophesy in Isaiah.

> And it shall come to pass in the last days, that the mountain
> of the Lord's house shall be established in the top of the
> mountains, and shall be exalted above the hills; and all
> nations shall flow into it.
>
> —Isaiah 2:2

Great things are happening in the body of Christ today. To be a partaker in the flow of power at this end time, you need a working faith. The Bible says there is nothing impossible for them that believed in God. I encouraged you today to be a part of this glorious end.

Let me end this chapter by showing you how the scripture described the great personalities we read about, what made them stand out, and what made them perform the great exploits recorded in their lives. I want you to understand that these people are like you. You have the same passion, but they achieved their purpose in life because of one distinguishing factor: faith.

> By faith, Enoch was translated that he should not see
> death; and was not found, because God had translated
> him; for before his translation he had this testimony, that
> he pleased God ...
> By faith, Noah, being warned of God of things not seen as
> yet, moved with fear, prepared an ark to the saving of his
> house; by which he condemned the world, and became
> heir of the righteousness which is by faith.
> By faith, Abraham, when he was called to go out into a
> place which he should after receive for an inheritance,
> obey; and he went out, not knowing whither he went.
> By faith, he sojourned in the land of promise, as in a
> strange country, dwelling in tabernacles with Isaac and
> Jacob, the heir with him of the same promise:

For he looks for a city which hath foundations, whose builder and maker is God.

Through faith, also Sarah herself received strength to conceive seed, and was delivered of a child when she was past age, because she judge him faithful who has promised ...

By faith, Abraham, when he was tried offered up Isaac: and he that had received the promises offered up his only begotten son.

Of whom it was said, "That in Isaac shall thy seed be called; Accounting that God was able to raise him up, even from the dead; from whence also he received him in a figure."

By faith, Isaac blessed Jacob and Esau concerning things to come.

By faith, Jacob, when he was a dying, blessed both the sons of Joseph; and worshiped, leaning upon the top of his staff.

By faith, Joseph, when he died, made mention of the departing of the children of Israel; and gave commandment concerning his bones.

By faith, Moses, when he was come to years, refused to be called the son of Pharaoh's daughter ...

By faith, the harlot Rahab perished not with them that believed not, when she had received the spies with peace.

And what shall I more say? For the time would fail me to tell of Gideon, and of Barak, and of Samson, and of Jephthah; of David also, and Samuel, and of the prophets;

Who through faith subdued kingdoms, wrought righteousness, obtained promises, stopped the mouths of lions.

Quenched the violence of fire, escaped the edge of the sword, out of weakness were made strong, waxed valiant in fight, turned to flight the armies of the aliens."

—Hebrews 11:5–34

Everything is possible with faith. Friends, it is by faith—and nothing else. Let your faith deliver your hope to you. If you have faith and work it, nothing will be impossible for you anymore. I see you on top of your world in Jesus's name.

Key Revelations from the Chapter

- ✓ Faith only works if we work it.
- ✓ Working your faith is simply synchronizing your beliefs with your confessions and actions.
- ✓ Walking in faith commands proof.
- ✓ God is not a respecter of persons, but he respects our faith.

Notes
My Learning Points

THE BRIDGE DESTROYERS

A bridge that connects two points, performing the function for which it was built, needed to be guided against things that can lead to its collapse. In order to guide and adequately protect the bridge, we need to know what things pose threats to the bridge. What can put the functionality of the bridge in jeopardy? What things are hazardous to the continual existence of the bridge? Besides taking adequate care of the bridge through proper maintenance and reinforcing weak points from time to time, you still have to know which things pose threats to the continual functioning of your bridge.

In the natural world, bridges can easily be put out of use or destroyed with explosives. We see this happening in war situations and times hostility. The enemy can target and destroy important bridges if their explosives are allowed to access them. These explosives come in different forms and potencies, and their destructive tendencies also vary by type.

The devil is in constant hostility with our walk with God. In this context, we will look at the things that can act as explosives against our faith. The devil is deploying arsenals every day to blow up our connection with the supernatural. If these explosives (faith destroyers) are not watched and guarded against, they can jeopardize our relationships with God. The enemy of people, satan is constantly targeting our faith with an arsenal of explosives.

Fear

The number one enemy of faith is fear. Faith and fear cannot coexist in the same heart. They are like light and darkness. The moment fear creeps into your heart, it eats up the faith. Fear glorifies the devil and attracts failure.

The spirit of fear comes from the prince of darkness. It came from the depths of hell. Living in fear is a life of enmity with God. It is a spirit that only produces failure. When God brings good news to His people, the messenger of the news usually says, "Fear not." This assurance is necessary because fearful hearts are unreceptive to the Word of God. The angel of the Lord told Zacharias not to be afraid when he brought the good news that his prayer for his barren wife had been answered.

> But the angel said unto him, fear not Zacharias; for thy prayer is heard; and thy wife Elizabeth shall bear thee a son, and thou shalt call his name John.
>
> —Luke 1:13

Friend, God has heard your prayers. The fear in your heart is hindering its physical manifestation. If God tells you not to fear, take him at His word. He is the Alpha and the Omega; He knows what He is talking about.

The good news is that God has not given us the spirit of fear. Therefore, whatever is not from God can be uprooted—and must be uprooted—for you to function in His purpose. Paul admonish Timothy not be fearful. There is a spirit behind fear that must be rooted up for faith to take hold in our heart.

> For God hath not given us the spirit of fear; but of power, and of love, and of sound mind.
>
> —2 Timothy 1:7

Fear creeps in as doubt. When doubt comes to you, it does not mean you have lost your faith; it only indicates the devil is doing his work. As a person of faith, you need to cast the doubt out of your mind by rebuking the devil. The Bible says the devil will flee from you if you rebuke him. However, if you allow doubt to linger in your mind more than necessary, it gives birth to fear, which replaces faith. Doubt is the first ingredient in the cycle of failure. It gives birth to fear, anxiety, and withholding from God. This results in closed heavens, failure, and more fear—and the cycle continues.

The easiest way the devil introduces fear into somebody's mind is with its cunning way of twisting the truth in the Word of God.

> Now the serpent was more cunning than any beast of the field which the Lord has made. And he said unto the woman, "Yea hath God said; 'Ye shall not eat of every tree of the garden?'"
> And the woman said unto the serpent, "We may eat of the fruit of the trees of the garden:

But of the fruit of the tree which is in the midst of the garden, God hath said, 'Ye shall not eat of it, neither shall ye touch it, least ye die.'"

And the serpent said unto the woman, "Ye shall not surely die:

For God doth know that in the day ye eat thereof, then your eyes shall be opened, and ye shall be as gods, knowing good and evil."

—Genesis 3:1–5

God commanded, "Of every tree of the garden you may freely eat; but of the tree of the knowledge of good and evil, you shall not eat, for in the day that you eat of it *you shall surely die.*"

The devil came and twisted the truth by introducing *not* into God's statement. He did not stop there. He went ahead and told the woman what God had not told them—giving them a promise that is already inherent in them from God. The devil told them they shall be as God, which in actual sense was what they were. The devil is cunning, and he is a trickster. His tricks have not changed. He perverts every word you hear and destroys whatever faith you are building on the truth in the Word of God.

Fear is a poisonous arrow shot at the heart the moment you allow it to take seat. It creeps in subtly as a small question and grows to poison the entire system. What if this did not come to pass? Rather than say, "I know God can never lie," this seemingly harmless question of the Word of God can destroy your entire faith. Watch out!

The thief does not come except to steal and to kill and to destroy.

—John 10:10

If the devil brings doubt to your mind, remember that he is a thief. His three areas of specialization are stealing, killing, and destroying. He has nothing to offer other than deceit. He cannot help you do anything but destroy. He cannot add positively to you. He only adds burdens. If you soak yourself with this truth, he cannot get to your faith. Moreover, we have the unwavering assurance of victory through the blood of Jesus Christ.

Worries and Anxiety

Worries and anxiety are terrific faith killers. They are cancerous cells in the faith life of a believer. They destroy faith faster than any known disease can destroy the body. When they enter a believer, they do not give him the impression that something is wrong with his or her faith life.

A worried or anxious believer does not doubt the truthfulness of God's promise; he or she is apprehensive about when the promise will come to pass. Apart from the devil introducing fear to your mind through his twisting of the truth in the Word of God by way of doubt, you can also hurt yourself by allowing worries to overtake you. Worries and doubts are brothers; where you find one, you find the other. They both relate very well to their senior brother (fear).

> And God is able to make all grace abound toward you, that you, always having all sufficiency in all things, may have abundance for every good work.
> —2 Corinthians 9:8

Worries have no place in your life. The prescription against worry is as simple as what the scripture quoted above said. Through God's grace toward us, He brings our expectations to accomplishment.

Do you worry about what tomorrow will bring or what the next moment will bring? What help have any of your worries brought since you were born? They steal your health, kill your joy, kill your dependency and fellowship with God, and leave you impotent and incapacitated at the mercy of satan.

A French philosopher once said, "My life is full of many misfortunes that never happened." Are you worried about a situation exploding in your face? Who told you God is on holiday or comes late? Whatever God chooses to do is for his glory and your lifting. That is what is called faith.

When Lazarus was sick, they sent for Jesus. He did not come when Mary and Martha expected him to come, and Lazarus died. When Jesus was informed of his sickness, he told His disciples that the sickness was not unto death. The illness Lazarus faced was not capable of destroying him. I want you to learn something from this story: Jesus knew Lazarus would not die from his sickness, and he delayed in going to Bethany to heal him.

When Lazarus died and was buried, God was waiting to achieve two things with Lazarus: proving his awesome power to bring any dead situation back to life (thereby glorifying His name) and giving Lazarus an undeniable testimony.

After Lazarus was raised from the dead, anywhere Jesus go to preach, Lazarus would show up and sit by His side as a living testimony of God's glory. God uses any situation you are going through to glorify His name and bring a lifting for you in Jesus's name.

> Now a certain man was sick, named Lazarus, of Bethany, the town of Mary and her sister Martha.
> (It was that Mary which anointed the Lord with ointment and wiped his feet with her hair, whose brother Lazarus was sick.)

> Therefore his sisters sent unto him, saying, "Lord, behold, he whom thou lovest is sick."
> When Jesus heard that, he said, "This sickness is not unto death, but for the glory of God, that the Son of God might be glorified thereby."
>
> —John 11:1–3

Several destinies are in cages today because of worries. Instead of working yourself up, why don't you approach your Father in heaven through prayers with faith and prove his words. Apostle Paul in one of his epistles wrote:

> Be anxious for nothing, but in everything by prayer and supplication, with thanksgiving, let your requests be made known to God.
>
> —Philippians 4:6

Jesus knew how destructive worries are to our faith and took time to teach His disciples about this very important subject.

> And he said unto his disciples; "Therefore I say unto you, take no thought for your life, what ye shall eat; neither for the body, what ye shall put on.
> The life is more than meat, and the body more than raiment. Consider the ravens: for they neither sow nor reap; which neither have storehouse nor barn; and God feedeth them: how much more are ye better than the fowls?
> And which of you with taking thought can add to his stature one cubit?
> If ye then be not able to do that thing which is least, why take ye thought for the rest?

Consider the lilies how they grow: they toil not, they spin not; and yet I say unto you, that Solomon in all his glory was not arrayed like one of these.

If God so clothe the grass, which is today in the field, and tomorrow is cast into the oven; how much more will he clothe you, O ye of little faith?

And seek not ye what ye shall eat, or what ye shall drink, neither be ye of doubtful mind.

For all these things do the nations of the world seek after: and your father knoweth that ye have need of these things?"

—Luke 12:22–30

And which of you with taking thought can add to his stature one cubit? Worries take you nowhere positive. They march you toward hell. They have no benefits and are unproductive. They cannot add to your status. Why engage in such a time-wasting venture? Put your attention and trust on the last sentence of the text: *And your Father knoweth that ye have need of these things.*

Praise God. My Father in heaven knows that I need to be blessed financially. He knows I need to be in good health. He knows I desire every good thing that life has to offer—and He is more than able to provide them for me. Why should I allow worries to take me away from pleasing Him and receiving my rewards? I want you to boldly make this declaration: *Worries, you have no place in my life from today onward, in the mighty name of Jesus.*

Wrong Label

Another faith destroyer is a wrong label. This is people's distorted opinions of you and being unable to see what you are capable of doing.

People see you and call you names from your past. They use what you were yesterday to relate to you today—and possibly tomorrow.

Friend, I want to assure you that they only know who you were yesterday—and possibly this moment—but they are at a loss about what God has in store for you tomorrow. Yesterday is in the past. It is already consigned to history. Nothing can change your yesterday, but God is more interested in your tomorrow. Thank Him for what He has done in your life so far. Key in through faith what he is about to do now and in the future. Don't allow the label of smallness they have put on you to limit your destiny. After all, the people who put this label on you are not God. Why would you allow their counsels to come true in your life? Stand up to them. Say no. I have a glorious future. God is taking me to my expected end. Where God is taking you has already been decided. When you enter it is determined by your faith in God.

When David appeared at the battleground to visit his brothers, the Philistine captain was busy tormenting the armies of God day and night. When David saw Goliath, his faith in God was kindled. He could see God delivering the giant into his hand and began to make inquiries as to what rewards awaited whoever could defeat Goliath and take away the reproach. But his brother (Eliab) could only see David as a mere shepherd boy. However, in God's agenda and design, David was a future king of Israel.

One of the steps that would take David to the throne was confronting the giant in battle. His brothers didn't know it or understand it. David worked in tandem with God's plan to walk his faith by taking on Goliath and actualizing his purpose in life.

Beware of what people see and say about you. If it is not in line with the Word of God, then it is a lie from the pit of hell. You may not be able to stop them from seeing or saying what they choose to see or say about you, but you have the power to not believe them, which limits your destiny in Christ. What God sees and says about you is the only thing that will come to pass. Guide your faith jealously because you cannot please God without it.

> And David left his supplies in the hand of the supply keeper, ran to the army,
> And came and greeted his brothers.
> Then as he talked with them, there was the champion, the Philistine of Gath
> Goliath by name, coming up from the armies of the Philistines; and he spoke
> according to the same words. So David heard them.
> ... Then David spoke to the men who stood by him, saying, "What shall be
> Done for the man who kills this Philistine and take away the reproach from Israel?
> For who is this uncircumcised Philistine, that he should defy the armies of the living God?
> Now Eliab his oldest brother heard when he spoke to the men; and Eliab's anger was aroused against David, and he said, "Why did you come down here?
> And with whom have you left those few sheep in the wilderness? I know your pride and the insolence of your heart, for you have come down to see the battle."
> —1 Samuel 17:22–29(NKJV)

David's faith was alive in him; he knew God's capabilities. He also knew he was more than able to deliver the Philistine champion into his hand. Eliab saw his brother as a mere shepherd boy, and that was the label he put on David. David did not let the perception of his brother limit him or allow it to destroy his faith in God. He refused to accept his brother's verdict concerning him. He knew that the people could only see his past. He put his trust in God to deliver the giant into his hand, which was precisely what God did. Friend, you have to be careful about allowing what people say about you to permeate your mind and affect your faith.

The same thing happened to our Lord Jesus in Nazareth where He was brought up. The people were looking at His yesterday and asking, "Is this not Joseph's son?" Their question was meant to reduce His divinity and make Him a mere mortal. Refuse to take their verdict because it is just a figment of their imagination, and it can never be the true picture of who you are.

> God forbid; yea, let God be true, but every man a liar; as it is written, "That thou mightest be justified in thy sayings, and mightest overcome when thou art judged."
> —Romans 3:4

You have the choice of accepting their verdict or rejecting it. Nothing can be forced on your destiny without your permission. The moment they pronounce the label they have on you, refuse their verdict and exercise your faith. The good results God will deliver to your hand through your faith will change their minds about you.

They labeled Jesus as a mere son of Joseph the carpenter in His hometown, so much so that they could not receive from Him. Despite showing them who he was in Isaiah, from the book of prophets, the people clung to the label they already had on him instead of taking advantage of the supernatural in Jesus.

> So He came to Nazareth, where He had been brought up, and as His custom was, He went into the synagogue on the Sabbath day and stood up to read.
> And He was handed the book of the prophet Isaiah. And when He had opened the book, He found the place it was

written: "The Spirit of the Lord is upon me because He has
anointed me to preach the gospel to the poor,

He has sent Meme to heal the brokenhearted, to proclaim
liberty to the captives and recovery of sight to the blind,
to set at liberty those who are oppressed; to proclaim the
acceptable year of the Lord."

Then He closed the book, and gave it back to the attendant
and sat down. And the eyes of all who were in the
synagogue were fixed on Him.

And He began to say to them, "Today this scripture is
fulfilled in your hearing."

So all bore witness to Him, and marveled at the gracious
words that proceeded out of His mouth. And they said. "Is
this not Joseph's son?"

—Luke 4:16–22

Jesus, carrying the Spirit of God, was in a position to set free
everyone under the oppression of the devil. The people could not
see His divinity, and they limited Him with a label. In the scripture
quoted above, Jesus rebuked the people instead of accepting the label
placed on him. You need to be prepared for people's violent reactions
whenever you refuse the label they have for you. They seek to destroy
Jesus because he rebukes them for the wrong label being put on Him.

Beloved, the responsibility rests squarely on your shoulder. You
will permit faith destroyers to have a place in your life—or you won't.
Arise today, say no more to the manipulations of the devil, gird your
loins with the shield of faith, and see God's reward.

Above all, taking the shield of faith, wherewith ye shall be
able to quench all the fiery darts of the wicked.

—Ephesians 6:16

Your faith is a potent weapon for conquering the devil. He knows this, and that is why he will stop at nothing to see that you don't have it or you lose the one you already had. Friend, I encourage you to watch out for faith destroyers pointed out in this chapter. You can be sure of victory in Jesus's name.

Key Revelations from the Chapter

- ✓ There are things that can harm or destroy your faith.
- ✓ Some of these faith destroyers are fear, anxiety, and wrong labels.
- ✓ Your faith is the target of the enemy of humankind (satan).
- ✓ Faith destroyers, such as fear, are from the pit of hell.
- ✓ You need to recognize and guard against these faith destroyers.

Notes
My Learning Points

BENEFITS OF FAITH

Blessed be the Lord, who daily loadeth us with
benefits, even the God of our salvation.
—Psalm 68:19

The Lord our God is preoccupied with loading us with His benefits. His thoughts toward us are good and not evil. His thoughts toward us include giving us an expected end halleluiah! God is a rewarder of those who seek him, and we can only seek Him through faith. The Bible says it is impossible to please God without faith. When you have faith, God is pleased and commands His blessings upon your life.

When Jesus saw the faith of the man sick with palsy and the four people that brought him to be healed, He immediately loaded him with benefits that can be placed under two categories: positional and conditional benefits. Jesus changed the man positionally and conditionally.

> When Jesus saw their faith, he said unto the sick of the palsy, "Son, thy sins be forgiven thee."
> But there were certain of the scribes sitting there, and reasoning in their hearts,
> Why doth this man thus speak blasphemies? Who can forgive sins but God only?

And immediately when Jesus perceived in his Spirit that
they so reasoned within themselves, he said unto them,
"Why reason ye these things in your hearts?
Whether is it easier to say to the sick of the palsy, 'Thy sins
be forgiven thee,' or to say, 'Arise, and take up thy bed,
and walk?'
But that ye may know that the Son of man hath power on
earth to forgive sins, (he saith to the sick of the palsy,)
I say unto thee, Arise, and take up thy bed, and go thy way
into thine house."

—Mark 2:5–11

Positional Benefit of Faith

The first benefit we receive from faith is forgiveness of sins. When
you move with faith to receive the Lord Jesus Christ as the Lord and
Savior of your life, He redeemed you of your sins through the grace
available in His shed blood. Your salvation is procured by grace
through faith. It takes the mixture of grace and faith to be saved.
God's grace abounds; it's available all the time, but it takes Him
seeing your faith for the grace to be released.

For the grace of God that bringeth salvation hath appeared
to all men.

—Titus 2:11

For we are saved by hope: but hope that is seen is not hope;
for what a man seeth, why doth he yet hope for?

—Romans 8:24

When we are born again, we are translated from the kingdom of
darkness into light. We change positionally from being a slave to sin

into a position of sonship with God and become a joint heir with Christ in the heavenly places. Through salvation, we become citizens of heaven (the supernatural), and we are no more of the flesh (the natural).

Our position in the scheme of things changes, and the way we do things changes. We are no more of the flesh; we are of the spirit. Our divine nature is kindled, and we begin to operate as the spirit people we are. I call this *positional transformation*. Positional transformation is a huge benefit. When we change positionally, we are no longer in the camp of losers. The eternal condemnation we are clothed with due to sin is replaced by glory through the redemption in Jesus's blood.

Our names are written in the Book of Life, and we are candidates of heaven. As a born-again child of God, God orders your steps. Your dominion is restored, and your former reprobate mind is replaced by the mind of Christ.

> For who has known the mind of the Lord, that he may instruct him? But we have the mind of Christ.
> —1 Corinthians 2:16

Positional benefit is the first line of benefit faith offers to a believer. When we are changed positionally in Christ, we become candidates for conditional changes and benefits.

Conditional Benefits of Faith

Conditional benefits of faith are numerous. They encompass all the blessings God promised in His words. When your faith is in place, you harvest these promises and reflect the perfect image of God. Appropriating conditional benefits of faith depends on your knowledge and understanding of them. You need to know they exist and have a grasp of their workability. This is what is commonly referred to as the *principles of the kingdom.*

Man does not create principles or natural and spiritual laws. For instance, people did not create the law of gravity. Sir Isaac Newton discovered them, and he used the understanding of their workability to the advantage of humankind. Every principle needs to be discovered and understood for you to take advantage of them. Christians operating with little faith are candidates for positional benefits of faith only. If you step up your level of faith, discover what God is saying, and release your faith in line with these words, nothing can stop you from appropriating the words (promises).

Faith is taking God by His word, acting on the Word of God, and believing that the Word of God cannot fail. What you see in the Word of God brings hope to your life. The hope you wait on is your demonstration of faith.

Before going into specific examples of conditional benefits of faith, let me take time to open your eyes to how you can reap God's promises through His Word. God speaks through the scriptures. His words are captured in the Holy Bible. Sometimes He drops an insight into your heart or speaks to you in dreams. In many of these occasions, the insights or dreams are validated in the Holy Bible.

In order to appropriate the Word of God, you need to discover it, understand it, and get a revelation from it. There is a spirit behind every word recorded in the scripture. This spirit gives the Word of God the power to perform and transform lives. This is the reason why only those who already enjoy positional benefits of faith are qualified for conditional benefits. However, if you are positionally changed but fail to discover and understand and get revelation about what God is saying concerning a situation, then the situation will not turn for you. This is the reason why a born-again, heaven-bound Christians can still be tormented by the devil with sickness, poverty, and his other vices.

There are always three parts to everything God says in our lives. Every word has the part that God will do, the part that we must do, and the benefit associated with it. The part that God will do is a settled part. By speaking the Word of God, he had already fulfilled His part. All the necessary ingredients and power for the Word of God to perform were already deposited inside it. The Word of God is a moving force; there is no power from hell that can break it or stop it.

> For as the rain cometh down, and the snow from heaven, and return not thither, but watereth the earth, and maketh it bring forth and bud, that it may give seed to the sower, and bread to the eater;
> So shall my Word be that goeth forth out of my mouth; it shall not return unto me void, but it shall accomplish that which I please, and it shall prosper in the thing whereto I sent it."
>
> —Isaiah 55:10–11

Doing your part is believing in what God said and walking in that belief. This involves believing with your heart what God has promised and confessing with your mouth the truth in the Word of God after taking care of the rationals. Taking care of the rationals involves walking in line with God's instructions in the promise. There are things that God will not do for you. I want you to know that God will not do for you what you can do for yourself. For example, God will not make a choice for you. That is why you are different from other creatures. God gave you a mind and free will to make your choices. The Holy Spirit lives in you and guides you in making good choices.

I call heaven and earth to record this day against you, that
I have set before you life and death, blessing and cursing;
therefore choose life, that both thou and thy seed may live.

—Deuteronomy 30:19

Not taking care of the rationals is like tempting God. It is like when Jesus encountered the devil.

Then the devil taketh him up into the holy city, and setteth
him on a pinnacle of the temple,
And saith unto him, if thou be the Son of God, cast thyself
down; for it is written, he shall give his angels charge
concerning thee; and in their hands they shall bear thee
up, lest at any time thou dash thy foot against a stone.
Jesus said unto him, "It is written again, 'Thou shall not
tempt the Lord thy God.'"

—Matthew 4:5–7

Don't abrogate your responsibility by saying you are exercising faith. For instance, you don't walk across the highway blindfolded and say, "By faith, I won't get knocked down by a moving vehicle." You don't wake up in the morning with faith that God will give you a shower. You have to get up, go to the bathroom, and take your bath. God will not do for you what you can do for yourself. If you are looking for a job, you have to prepare your resume and get it out.

Every Word of God has a benefit associated with it. There are words on healing with benefit of healing associated with them. There are words on prosperity with prosperity benefits associated with them. For whatever area you want a conditional benefit to be released to you, locate a word or words in that area and release your faith. The result will not be denied unto you.

Let us consider some example of conditional benefits you can connect with. The list is inexhaustible. The psalmist says He loads us with His benefits every day. Every new day brings fresh benefits. Receive yours now in the name of Jesus.

> Blessed be the Lord, who daily loadeth us with benefits, even the God of our salvation.
>
> —Psalm 68:19

Benefit of Prosperity

One of the conditional benefits of faith is prosperity. The word *prosperity* is loosely used to represent material wealth. But prosperity in the kingdom of God is an all-encompassing word. It represents state of wellness in the spirit, soul, and body. In other words, prosperity covers spiritual, mental, and physical well-being. Lacking in any of these areas brings about distortion and is not of God.

> Beloveth, I wish above all things that thou mayest prosper and be in health, even as thy soul prospereth.
>
> —3 John 1:2

It is the will of God for us to be made whole in spirit, soul, and body.

> And the very God of peace sanctify you wholly; and I pray God your whole spirit and soul and body be preserved blameless unto the coming of our Lord Jesus Christ.
>
> —1 Thessalonians 5:23

It is your redemptive right to prosper; anything contrary to this is not from God. However, if you are faced with little affliction, God will come through for you.

But my God shall supply all your needs according to his
riches in glory by Christ Jesus.

—Philippians 4:19

You have a good and faithful father who delights in your well-being.
God's mind is constantly good, and it never conceives of evil. Holy
God loves us with unquantifiable and unparalleled love. Beloved, see
what God says concerning you.

And all these blessings shall come on thee, and overtake
thee, if thou shalt hearken unto the voice of the Lord
thy God.
Blessed shall thou be in the city, and blessed shall thou be
in the field.
Blessed shall be the fruit of thy body, and the fruit of thy
ground, and the fruit of thy cattle, the increase of thy kine,
and the flocks of thy sheep.
Blessed shall be thy basket and thy store.
Blessed shalt thou be when thou comest in, and blessed
shalt thou be when thou goest out.

—Deuteronomy 28:2–6

According to the *Theological Workbook, bless* in both Hebrew and
Greek means to imbue with power for success, prosperity, fecundity,
and longevity. It means this power is inherent in you. God gave it to
you. You can only stir them up and exercise them if you are a person
of faith.

Benefit of Healing

Healing is receiving soundness into our feeble bodies. Humankind
is in continuous battle with the devil, and those in battle sometimes

sustain injuries. Sustaining an injury in a battle does not mean you have lost the battle. An injury might come as a result of carelessness on your part that the enemy (satan) took advantage of. The intensity of a battle can bring weariness to the body. All these injuries accumulate to bring some state of unsoundness to the body of the believer, but praise God, there is word that brings healing when faced with this situation.

> But he was wounded for our transgressions, he was bruised for our iniquities; the chastisement of our peace was upon him; and with his stripes we are healed.
> —Isaiah 53:5

Jesus Christ took those bashing on His body on His way to the cross. He was beaten to the point that his entrails were hanging out with stripes all over Him. Every sickness in this world that the devil could afflict people with has already been taken care by those stripes. To receive the conditional benefits, you need to believe that you were healed by His stripes—and your healing will come.

There is healing in the Word of God.

> He sent his Word and healed them, and delivered them from their destructions.
> —Psalm 107:20

If you desire healing in any area of your body today, locate a word from God and have an understanding of it. It will give you revelations, and with your faith in place, it will accomplish that which it is sent forth in Jesus's name. The Word of God is a healing balm and our Lord Jesus is the greatest physician. Prophet Jeremiah lamented when he saw prevailing ill health in Israel:

> Is there no balm in Gilead; is there no physician there?
> Why then is not the health of the daughter of my people
> recovered?
>
> Jeremiah 8:22

The good news is that there is still balm in Gilead and a physician is still there. The Word of God is the balm in Gilead and is eternal. Jesus Christ is the physician there and He is the same yesterday, today and forever.

Benefit of Favor

Favor is receiving a blessing that you are not ordinarily qualified to receive. Favor is succeeding where others are failing. Have you not noticed that there are people who are probably working the same job with the same education, but one is more blessed than the other? That is favor speaking in the life of that person. Friend, favor is what gives you the edge over your contemporaries. Don't despise it.

> And Joseph found favor in his sight and he served him;
> and he made him overseer over his house, and that he had
> he put into his hand.
> —Genesis 39:4 (American Standard Version)

Joseph joined the workforce of Potiphar through slavery, but by favor, he became overseer ahead of other slaves he met. Favor will get you promoted ahead of your seniors. It sets you apart. It is of the Lord to favor His own, and we learned earlier that you can only please Him through faith. If God is pleased with you, part of the reward you get is divine favor.

> For they got not the land in possession by their own sword, neither did their own arm save them; but thy right hand, and thy arm, and the light of thy countenance, because thou hadst favor unto them.
> —Psalm 44:3 (American Standard Version)

Stop and pray this prayer now. *God, I believe your word that says you will show mercy to those whom you chose to show mercy. Have mercy on me—and give me favor in all areas of my life in the name of your Son, Jesus Christ. Amen.*

I see favor coming upon you this week, this month, this year, and forever in Jesus's name.

Benefit of Longevity

Beloved, to live a long and fruitful life is a benefit from God. Our lives are in the hands of God. He is the giver of life, and he keeps and preserves it. When God is pleased with you, He gives you the benefit of long life.

Enoch never tasted death because he pleased God. God took him away and did not allow him to have the experience of death that is needed for separation from one realm to another.

> With long life will I satisfy him, and show him my salvation.
> —Psalm 91:16

Jehovah satisfied His beloveds with long life. Are you one of His beloveds? Your answer should be yes if you are operating with the kingdom faith. Otherwise, you need to make a conscious effort to develop faith in God now.

What is the use of being blessed, being highly successful, and having plenty of gold and silver if you don't live long enough to enjoy it? Remember the story of the foolish, rich man in the Bible? After acquiring all the wealth in the world, he told himself it was time to sit back, relax, and enjoy, but God demanded his soul that same night.

> And he spake a parable unto them, saying, "The ground of a certain rich man brought forth plentifully."
> And he thought within himself saying, "What shall I do; because I have no room where to bestow my fruits?"
> And he said, "This will I do: I will pull down my barns, and build greater; and there will I bestow all my fruits and my goods.
> And I will say to my soul; soul thou hast much goods laid up for many years; take thine ease, eat, drink, and be merry."
> But God said unto him, "Thou fool, this night thy soul shall be required of thee, then whose shall those things be, which thou hast provided?"
>
> —Luke 12:16–20

Key Revelations from the Chapter

- ✓ Living and walking in faith commands benefits from heaven.
- ✓ Faith grants you positional benefits.
- ✓ It transfers you from the kingdom of darkness to the kingdom of light.
- ✓ Faith confers conditional blessings.
- ✓ These conditional benefits include prosperity, healing, favor, and long life.

Notes
My Learning Points

The Place of the Blood

The necessary resource for building this connecting bridge to the supernatural is totally encapsulated in the blood of Jesus Christ. In essence, the faith this book is discussing is based on the redemptive work. Jesus Christ redeemed us by shedding His blood on the cross of Calvary.

It will cost you nothing to build the connecting bridge because Christ already paid the price with His precious blood. Salvation comes from grace through faith; it is not by our works. Just believe in Him and what He accomplished for you on the cross.

Following the fall of humankind in the Garden of Eden, people became disconnected from the supernatural. They were given to a reprobate mind, and the scripture made us understand that humankind died spiritually that day. We became sin and unrighteous and lost the ability to put our minds to full use as designed by God.

> The wages of sin is death; but the gift of God is eternal life through Jesus Christ.
>
> —Romans 6:23

> Reprobate silver shall men call them, because the Lord hath rejected them.
>
> —Jeremiah 6:30

And even as they did not like to retain God in their
knowledge, God gave them over to a reprobate mind, to
do those things which are not convenient.

—Romans 1:28

Examine yourselves, whether ye be in the faith; prove your
own selves, know ye not your own selves, how that Jesus
Christ is in you, except ye be reprobates?

—2 Corinthians 13:5

The repercussion of operating with a reprobate mind is suicidal,
which is seen in these scriptures. However, God did not want humans
to perish in such a pitiable condition, and he designed a way out for
them through the shedding of the innocent blood of His Son. Jesus
Christ's blood made a final atonement for the sins of men and women.

Christ came on the scene to rescue you and me from the fangs
of death. He came for a renewal of our minds; he exchanged His
righteousness for our unrighteousness on the cross. He took our
sins upon himself so we could become whole and acceptable before
His Father in heaven. What a clear demonstration of His love for
wretched sinners like us!

God has demonstrated His love for fallen humans since the
Garden of Eden. When Adam fell, God make a sacrifice of atonement
on behalf of humankind and used the skin of the slayed animal to
cover Adam's nakedness. God drove Adam and Eve out of the garden
so that they would not put their hands on the Tree of Life and eat of it.
He also brought fulfillment to His pronouncement on them following
the disobedience of His instruction.

And unto Adam he said, "Because thou hast hearkened
unto the voice of thy wife, and hast eaten of the tree, of
which I commanded thee saying, Thou shalt not eat of:

Cursed is the ground for thy sake; in sorrow shalt thou eat
of it all the days of thy life;

Thorns also and thistles shall it bring forth to thee; and
thou shalt eat of the herb of the field;

In sweat of thy face shalt thou eat bread, till thou return
unto the ground; for out of it was thou taken: for dust thou
art, and unto dust shalt thou return."

And Adam called his wife name Eve because she was the
mother of all living.

Unto Adam also and to his wife did the Lord God make
coats of skins, and clothed them.

And the Lord God said, "Behold, the man is become as one
of us, to know good and evil: and now, lest he put forth
his hand, and take also of the tree of life, and eat, and live
forever."

Therefore the Lord God sent him forth from the Garden of
Eden, to till the ground from whence he was taken.

—Genesis 3:17–23

Sin disconnected men and women from the presence of God. For them to approach God's presence, sin needed to be blotted out. This was achieved with blood sacrifice. We saw this with the first offspring from Adam and Eve. Cain and Abel pursued God in worship and offerings.

We also saw the offering of bulls for the atonement of sin by the high priest on behalf of the people during the old covenant of the Law. People are in a constant fallen state with sin, and they needed to continually shed blood to cover up for their sins so they could approach God in fellowship. All these sacrifices of animals to cover human sins were shadows of what Jesus Christ did on the cross at Calvary.

Jesus paid the final price so that our sins in the past, present, and future would be blotted out once and for all. He ushered us into the righteousness of God through grace by this offering. That was why He said, "It is finished." The faith to connect with the supernatural presented in this book was made possible through this same grace. This grace was a gift from God to people because of His love for us.

> For God so loved the world that he gave his only begotten
> Son, that whosoever believeth in him should not perish,
> but have everlasting life.
>
> —John 3:16

It takes belief in Jesus Christ to be a beneficiary of this grace. Your works, actions, and inactions cannot usher you into it. Scripture described this era of grace (unmerited favor) as the New Covenant. Everything Jesus did on the cross at Calvary redeemed us and reconciled us permanently to our Father in heaven to represent the New Covenant.

Under the New Covenant, God recognized the weakness in you and me and absolved us from the work that is necessary for redemption.

> But now hath he obtained a more excellent ministry, by how much also he is the mediator of a better covenant, which was established upon better promises.
> For if that first covenant had been faultless, and then should no place have been sought for the second.
> For finding fault with them, he saith, "Behold, the day come, saith the Lord, when I will make a new covenant with the house of Israel and with the house of Judah.
> Not according to the covenant I made with their fathers in the day when I took them by hand to lead them out of the land of Egypt; because they continued not in my covenant, and I regarded them not," saith the Lord.

"For this is the covenant that I will make with the house
of Israel after those days," saith the Lord; "I will put my
laws into their mind, and write them in their hearts: and
I will be to them a God, and they shall be to me a people:
And they shall not teach every man his neighbor, and
every man his brother, saying, Know the Lord: for all shall
know me, from the least to the greatest.
For I will be merciful to their unrighteousness, and their
sins and their iniquities will I remember no more."
In that he saith, "A new covenant, he hath made the first
old. Now that which decayeth and waxeth old is ready to
vanish away."

—Hebrews 8: 6–13

Praise God! What a better covenant we have in Jesus. Brethren, you
can only be a partaker in this New Covenant through your belief and
faith in Jesus Christ. I want to make a distinction between belief and
faith in Jesus Christ. The Bible says demons also believed, but their
own belief was not unto salvation.

If you say, "Yes, I believed Jesus came to the world, He was the Son
of Mary, and God did use Him to perform miracles," this is not the
kind of belief I'm talking about. To be part of the New Covenant
and be a candidate (heir) to the throne of God and beneficiary of the
goodies contained in redemption, your belief system and faith must
be on the authenticity of the finished work of Jesus Christ on the
cross of Calvary, His shed blood that washed you clean of your sins
and iniquities. Accept His lordship over your life and then—bravo!—
you are there to link up with the supernatural and see a physical
manifestation of God's glory in your life.

Key Revelations from the Chapter

✓ Redemption through the blood of Jesus is the necessary resource to build faith.

✓ We are under the dispensation of the new covenant.

✓ Under the new covenant we are made righteous not by works but by grace.

✓ To be part of the glorious new covenant you have to invite and accept Jesus Christ to be the Lord over your life.

Notes
My Learning Points

THE FINAL WORD

Beloved, being in Christ is the best experience anybody can have in this world. In fact, whatever you seem to be enjoying right now if you are outside His banner cannot be compared with the righteousness, peace, and joy in the Holy Ghost that He wants to give to you if you come to Him. Christ wants to come to your life so that He can transform you and make you a new person. This can only happen if you change your mind about being indifferent to His call and open your heart for Him to come in. When He comes into your life, you will begin to experience heaven on earth, and the kingdom of heaven will be inside of you. This is the kingdom of heaven He spoke about.

> And saying, "Repent ye; for the kingdom of heaven is at hand."
>
> —Matthew 3:2

Without Christ, life is full of crises. In fact, the Bible made us understand that we are condemned without Him in our lives. Without the remission of sin through His shed blood on the cross of Calvary, there is no basis for faith. Only faith through His accomplished work on the cross can make us please God.

In essence, without Christ in your life, you cannot connect with the supernatural. Don't be deceived. Any other faith they preach to you outside of Jesus Christ is sinking sand that cannot endure or withstand the test of time. However, if you heed His call today and accept Him into your life, you are likened to a wise man who builds his house upon the rock.

> Therefore whosoever heareth these sayings of mine, and doeth them, I will liken him unto a wise man, which built his house upon the rock;
> And the rain descended, and the floods came, and the winds blew, and beat upon that house; and it fell not: for it was founded upon a rock.
> And everyone that heareth these sayings of mine, and doeth them not, shall be likened unto a foolish man, which built his house upon the sand:
> And the rain descended, and the flood came, and the winds blew, and beat upon that house; and it fell: and great was the fall of it.
> —Matthew 7:24–27

Friend, the rain will always fall, the flood will always come, and the winds will blow and beat upon us in this life and upon our faith. Only those whose faith is built upon the rock (Jesus Christ) can withstand the trials of life. Life will always present challenges. You can't run away from this, but there is victory in Jesus Christ

> These things I have spoken unto you, that in me ye might have peace. In the world ye shall have tribulation: but be of good cheer; I have overcome the world.
> —John 16:33

We hear and read about people committing suicide these days over small trials in life. Some of the victims of these devilish antics are at the peaks of their careers. Do you wonder what is going on? These people's faith is built on the sinking sand and not the rock—and that is why they fall when a little storm beats against them.

Friend, seek Jesus today. He is the solution to every problem in life—with no exceptions.

> There was a man of the Pharisees, named Nicodemus, a ruler of the Jews.
> The same came to Jesus by night, and said unto him, Rabbi, we know that thou art a teacher come from God; for no man can do these miracles that thou doest, except God be with him.
> Jesus answered and said unto him, "Verily, verily, I say unto thee, 'Except a man be born again, he cannot see the kingdom of God.'"
>
> —John 3:1–3

To be born again means renewal of your spirit through Christ. I have experienced the beauty in Christ firsthand. I have seen folks who had been written off, but they turned around miraculously when they encountered Jesus. He wants to give you beauty for ashes, the oil of joy for mourning, and the garment of praise for the spirit of heaviness.

The same Jesus is calling on you today. He says come, and I will make you. He called Simon Peter and Andrew to follow him and make them fishers of men. These common, unlearned people were turned into celebrities. He is calling on you the same way today.

> And Jesus, walking by the Sea of Galilee, saw two brethren; Simon called Peter, and Andrew his brother, casting a net into the sea; for they were fishers.
> And he saith unto them, "Follow me, and I will make you fishers of men."
>
> —Matthew 4:18–19

He says I am knocking at the door of your heart. If you can open it, I will come in. If you heed this call—no matter how terrible the situation—he will forgive you for all your sins and iniquities and give you a fresh breath of life, a new purpose, and a new direction. You will begin to experience life from a different perspective—one that is full of glory and honor.

Jesus is not coming into your life to condemn you. He is coming to give you eternal life, abundant life, and peace that pass all understanding.

> "Come now, and let us reason together," saith the Lord: "though your sins be as scarlet, they shall be as white as snow; though they be red like crimson, they shall be as wool."
>
> —Isaiah 1:18

Consider the story of Saul of Tarsus. He was persecuting and jailing all who believed in Jesus. On his murderous journey to Damascus, he encountered the Lord, and his story changed. All his past deeds were forgiven, and he was elected an apostle of the Lord Jesus.

Don't allow the devil to continue to have a better part of you. You have a glorious part in Jesus. If you want to enter into that part right now, say these little prayers.

> Lord Jesus, I recognize that I'm a sinner and cannot help myself. That is why I have come to you today for help. Cleanse me with your precious blood, which you shed on the cross of Calvary for my sake. I accept you as my Lord and Savior today. Come into my life and direct my path. I know I'm joined with you in the kingdom of your Father, in Jesus's name.

Congratulations! You made it. You escaped from hell into the love of Jesus Christ. Your life has taken a positive turn in Jesus's mighty name. I want to encourage you to find a true Bible-believing church to fellowship with God's people. The anointed words you will be feeding on through this fellowship will sharpen and deepen your knowledge of God, and your faith shall come alive.

> Iron sharpeneth iron; so a man sharpeneth the countenance of his friend.
>
> —Proverbs 27:17

As you fellowship with God's people, they will build up your faith—and your life will never be the same. Beloved, one immediate thing you will begin to enjoy from Jesus is His peace.

> Peace I leave with you. My peace I give to you; not as the world gives do I give to you. Let not your heart be troubled, neither let it be afraid.
>
> —John 14:27

The peace the scripture referred to here means *shalom* in the Hebrew lexicon. Shalom is described as completeness, safety, soundness (in body), welfare, health, prosperity, peace, quiet, tranquility, contentment, peaceful use of human relationships, peace with God (especially in covenant relationships), and peace from war. Wow! What a complete package this peace represents.

Can you picture the full implications of what it means to experience this peace in your life? Can you picture your life being free from regrets, anxieties, and worries? This is what this book presents to you. Now that you have received Jesus into your life and are building up your bridge to connect with the supernatural, receive His peace in the name of Jesus.

You are going to have a firsthand experience with Him too. I know what I'm talking about. I have been on the other side, but I am now enveloped and enjoying the love of Christ. You are welcome to board.

I'm waiting to celebrate your victory with you. If you want to share your personal experience of your encounter with Jesus through this book, please e-mail me (ahmedfatai@gmail.com).

God blesses you richly in Jesus's name. Amen.

About *Connecting the Supernatural*

This easy-to-read-and-understand revelation from heaven presents the mind of God concerning humankind in a simple form. It depicts God's plans and purpose for our life. God's original plan for us is to dominate, subdue, replenish, and be fruitful. There was no proviso for struggles, sickness, or failure.

The struggles and failure we see today are a result of disruption in the link between the natural and the supernatural. This book prescribes the remedy to this disruption. It explains the need to amend the disruption in order to connect with the supernatural and be restored to God's original plan.